To K & J from E
Feb '79

What is it like to swim with a shark every day?

Don C. Reed, head diver at California's Marine World/Africa USA, tells us in this suspenseful account of his experiences with the broadhead sevengilled sharks that lived at the aquarium—in particular the massive female he called Sevengill.

From the moment she arrived, the dangerous Sevengill captured Reed's imagination. She displayed a majestic calm, yet Reed knew her to be one of the most savage predators in the world. At first he kept a wary distance as he went about his underwater chores.

Months passed without real trouble, and Reed's initial fear of Sevengill changed to trust. Gradually he and the other divers grew comfortable with the sharks and even began to play with them—until violent events reminded them that sharks are not pets.

Through Reed's fascinating tale, we come to see that sharks are a force of nature that deserve our respect—not the blood-thirsty monsters of movie fame, but fierce and efficient hunters that play a vital role in ocean ecology.

Sevengill: The Shark and Me pulls us right into the water to swim alongside the author and his favorite shark—a gripping story for all fans of true-life nature adventure.

SEVENGILL

The Shark and Me

by DON C. REED

Illustrated by Pamela Ford Johnson

ALFRED A. KNOPF ⤳ *New York*
SIERRA CLUB • *San Francisco*

To the mother of my children,
great friend of all my life;
counselor, lover, and chief mischief-maker:
to JEANNIE, my wife.

The Sierra Club, founded in 1892 by John Muir, has devoted itself to the study and
protection of the earth's scenic and ecological resources—mountains, wetlands, woodlands,
wild shores and rivers, deserts and plains. The publishing program of the Sierra Club
offers books to the public as a nonprofit educational service in the hope that they may
enlarge the public's understanding of the club's basic concerns. The point of view expressed
in each book, however, does not necessarily represent that of the club. The Sierra Club
has some fifty chapters coast to coast, in Canada, Hawaii, and Alaska. For information
about how you may participate in its programs to preserve wilderness and the quality of
life, please address inquiries to Sierra Club, 730 Polk Street, San Francisco, CA 94109.

THIS IS A BORZOI BOOK PUBLISHED BY ALFRED A. KNOPF, INC.

Library of Congress Cataloging-in-Publication Data
Reed, Don C. Sevengill: the shark and me.
Includes index.
Summary: Don Reed, a diver at Marine World, reconstructs the birth and early life of
the shark known as Sevengill, describes his experiences with her, and recounts other un-
derwater adventures. 1. Sevengill (Shark)—Juvenile literature. 2. Reed, Don C.—Juve-
nile literature. 3. Sharks—United States—Biography—Juvenile literature. 4. Divers—
United States—Biography—Juvenile literature. [1. Sevengill (Shark) 2. Sharks. 3. Reed,
Don C.   4. Divers] I. Johnson, Pamela Ford, ill. II. Title.
QL795.S46R35 1986   597'.31   86-2727
ISBN: 0-394-86926-5   ISBN: 0-394-96926-X (lib. bdg.)

Acknowledgments

So many people deserve thanks and recognition: from Mike Demetrios, President of Marine World/Africa USA, who took out a second mortgage on his house to keep Marine World alive; to the author of every shark book I have read in a lifetime of looking; to Dave Di Fiore and Dennis Hada, photographers and friends; to editors Dinah Stevenson, Jenny Fanelli, and Laura Woodworth of Pantheon/Knopf and Diana Landau of Sierra Club Books for their intense creative involvement; to Fred Hill, my agent, who had faith in me before there was much reason to do so; to cousin Tom Snyder, who organized my relatives (too many to be individually named) and *bought me a word processor* (!) to write this book on; to fisherman Jeff Myers, Dave Powell, Director of Animal Husbandry at the Monterey Bay Aquarium, aquarist Ed Miller, and Director John McCosker of Steinhart Aquarium, who caught, cared for, and shared the shark called Sevengill with us; to Ken Shiels and Stan Minasian, for encouragement; to Dave Ebert, who did the only research I know of on sevengills in the wild; to John Rupp, Curator of Fishes at the Point Defiance Aquarium, Tacoma, Washington, for his correspondence and scientific paper on sevengills; to Abe Cunang, whose articles on shark fishing were so accurate and finely detailed; to all of the sixty-some divers I have worked with, but most especially Lindy Mitchell-Cook, John Racanelli, Keith Worcester, and Alan Therkelsen; to Desirée Don and Roman Jason Patrick Reed, my children, who give me joy every day of their lives; and to that individual without whom this book would not have been possible, Sevengill, the shark: thank you, very much.

Contents

A Note to the Reader

As a professional scuba diver for Marine World/Africa USA for thirteen years, I have spent approximately twelve thousand hours underwater, often in the company of various species of sharks.

This story is based on the life and adventures of one particular animal, a shark I knew as Sevengill. This was the name of her species (*Notorynchus cepedianus*, the broadhead sevengill shark), and also how I thought of her as an individual.

In writing this book I have had to fight the urge to exaggerate: to make the sharks appear more ferocious than they were, and to show myself as braver, stronger, wiser than I was. I am sure I have not always been successful; ego often colors memory.

Chapter 1 had to be fiction; no human eye was there to see when Sevengill was born, and first went hunting, and lived alone in the wild. In the remaining chapters, I have frequently jumped back and forth in time, rearranging the order in which events occurred, though not the incidents themselves.

Other than that, this story is true.

Don C. Reed
Fremont, California
October 1985

SEVENGILL
The Shark and Me

Pupo
Я что ред.

A Shark Is Born

~~~~~~

In the early summer of 1971, a very pregnant sevengill shark headed for the shallows of San Francisco Bay. It was time, and past time, for her babies to be born.

For more than two years the shark pups had grown inside her, changing from large yellow eggs to small brown sharks, nearly seven dozen of them, twelve to twenty inches long.

As they formed, the sharks had taken nourishment from the eggs. But now their food supply was gone, and the eighty-three unborn pups were starving. Unlike some shark species, these sevengilled sharks would not kill and eat each other in the womb; and not being mammals, they did not have umbilical cords to take food directly from their mother. If they did not come out into the world and catch their own food very soon, the pups would die unborn, and never know the sea.

Their birth had been delayed. For almost two months the bulging-bellied female had stopped the birth from happening, which is something pregnant sharks can do.

The reason was the winter rains.

The rains had pounded the earth that season, tearing off top-soil and fertilizer, tumbling tons of washed-off m··· k down the rivers to the delta and S~~ ~~~~~~~~~~ 'd the mud in the water make bre~~ ~~~~ sevengill shark's narrow gills, but ~~ ~~~~~ too much fresh water, which coulc ~~~~~~ r, ocean-going shark.

fresh water vs. salt water

For a while the pregnan ~~~~~~~~~~~ iark with black spots, had left the b ~~~~~~, cruising in the deeper, clearer waters of the Pacific Ocean outside the mouth of the natural harbor. Six weeks ago she had come back to her usual territory in the deep ships' channels of the bay. Since then she had been trying to reach the shallow mud flats in back of Candlestick Park, near the southwestern shore of the bay, where she herself had come into the world.

Fishermen called the spot she wanted "the Nursery" because it was the perfect place for a sevengill shark to be born. Here was an abundance of small food: fish called chimaeras, which looked like long-tailed swimming rabbits; bat rays with rich red meat; the spiny but slow and edible dogfish shark; and other ocean creatures a newborn shark might have a chance to catch. Also, and importantly, there were fewer large predators in the shallows to threaten the pups.

It would not be good for the babies to be born in the deep ships' channel where the female was now. The pups would not last an hour in this rough neighborhood. There were too many hunters here, like the mud shark with green eyes which now followed the sevengill.

She knew the mud shark was there, and she knew his size and

that he hunted. A sensitive organ called the lateral line, which ran along her side, could feel the different ripples that the mud shark made as he swam.

At first the pregnant shark pretended that the follower was not worth her notice. But when the second shark moved closer, the female abruptly yanked her head to one side, her jaws gaping in threat.

The smaller shark swerved off a few feet, but he did not go away. Normally he would not have dared to bother her, for fear of becoming a meal himself. But he was also curious, and he wondered (in the way of a shark) about the sevengill's swollen stomach. Was a birth about to happen? If some tender, juicy shark pups were going to be born soon, he would like to be there to greet them, with an open mouth.

The birth contractions began, quivering along the length of the powerful eight-foot female shark's body. She kept right on swimming, and this time she did not make the contractions stop as she had in the days before. Perhaps in some dim way she understood that the babies must be born now or they would die. If the silt had settled down in the shallows so that she could breathe the water, and if that portion of the sea was salty enough once more, she would do the birthing there. If not, the infant sharks would just have to be born wherever she was and take their chances.

She tried not to look like she was in a hurry. It was dangerous to act nervous or afraid in the presence of a predator. But when a thread of blood scent drifted from her, as the birth canal began to open, the follower instantly detected the scent and understood. As the bigger shark swam in toward the birthing grounds, the mud shark narrowed the distance between them.

Inside the stretchy-walled sac which was her mother's womb, Sevengill the shark lay very still, waiting to be born. In earlier days she and her eighty-two brothers and sisters had been quite active, as much as there was room to be, twitching their small, rough bodies, imitating the swim they would continue all their lives, practicing the gape of tiny jaws. But now, nothing. Every shark pup lay still, saving its energy.

Like the others, Sevengill was lined up with her head toward her mother's tail. She would have to be born headfirst. Her skin was covered not with scales but with thousands of tiny points called <u>denticles</u>, or skin teeth. They were all aimed backward so that Sevengill's hide was smooth one way and rough the other. If she were to go out of the womb tail first, the points of her skin would dig in and catch, and the pup would get stuck in the birth canal.

The pup waited. She was twenty inches long and fully formed. Sleek, powerful muscles stretched over her skeleton of cartilage, a softer, tougher substance than bone. A perfect little predator, she was ready to swim and fight or get away quick.

Now Sevengill scented something new: the natural chemicals her mother's body secreted to begin the birth—and a hint of the ocean, just outside. The doorway to the world had begun to open.

Up the deep ships' channel the pregnant shark hurried, uncaring now if she attracted attention, ready to fight if she had to. The babies must be born now, today, this hour! Her increased speed caused the liquid mud to accumulate on the insides of her throat, clogging the seven red fibrous gills on either side. She lowered her head sharply, which forced a jet of water through her gills, temporarily clearing them; that was how she coughed. She went on.

At last the ocean floor sloped upward, and the water if not clear was at least breathable. The female came to the end of the gouge in the seafloor that humans had carved to make room for their big ships. She hurried upward, into—

—the light. Her shadow showed beneath her as black water changed to gray and then to yellow. Her eyes withdrew into her skull, hiding for a second or two. This is how her species blinks, lacking the nictitating membrane that some sharks have like a sort of contact lens to shield the eye.

But if the change in light was strange to her, it was disaster for the shark who followed. The mud shark's green eyes are so delicate that his kind can seldom survive in an aquarium, where the eyeballs calcify from the light, turning white and hard until the shark dies.

With a swirl of frustrated rage, a movement so abrupt it was almost like swearing, the mud shark turned back to the dark and comfort of the deeps, where he presently forgot the seven-gill.

The mother shark continued several hundred yards farther, wanting a bit more distance from the drop-off to the deeps, lest something large be patrolling the edge.

She stopped. As if trying to bite her own tail, the birthing shark bent in upon herself.

Like giant hands the birth contractions squeezed the womb; Sevengill burst out into the sea.

Light, the first the baby shark had ever seen, shone blinding

all around. She yanked her eyeballs deep into her head. Everywhere roared first-felt sensations. Her nostrils were jammed with unfamiliar scents.

She fell onto the soft mud floor. For a moment, the twenty-inch shark just lay still, stunned by the strangeness all around. She yanked her jaws up and down to suck a little water down her throat to breathe, but this was an emergency procedure only. She needed to swim, to force seawater down her throat, so her gills could filter the oxygen out of the liquid she lived in. When

she stopped moving, so did the flow of oxygen-bearing water. Motion was her life.

She stretched her fins out like wings, letting them harden. They had been floppy soft for ease in birthing, but now they stiffened quickly. They had to. There wasn't time to lie around. This was no safe place.

Other little sharks landed beside her as the mother shark moved in figure eights above, dropping the brown, black-spotted pups out as she swam.

Something in Sevengill's mind told her she should get out of there quick. She was born knowing certain things without needing to be taught, as she would never have a teacher. One of these silent commands of instinct was to leave the scene of her birth. There would be hunting here, and soon.

She roused herself and moved off, beginning the swim she would continue all her life. Water pushed into her slightly open mouth and pulsed out through the gills in the walls of her throat. She breathed, and sensed the sea, and felt her muscles working smoothly; she swam as if she had practiced for years. The smear of mud where she'd hit the floor washed slowly off her broad, blunt snout. The motion that gave her breath would also keep her clean.

Then a splash came from above, and a diving bird burst by her, piercing its beak into the small, limp body of a stillborn, a shark for whom the birth had come too late. The bird, a cormorant, stabbed and struggled and swallowed underwater, so the nondiving gulls that whitened the surface above would not take her prey from her.

A face like a silver ghost loomed suddenly beside Sevengill. The cavernous mouth gaped—and the striped bass sucked the shark's body in, crossways. Sevengill's tail lashed desperately across his eyes and she broke free before the bass's throat teeth crushed her.

Then the sea lions came.

There were three of them. Humans would have thought them beautiful. Sleek and supple, the finest swimmers in the sea, they were strong enough to swim across an ocean. They could corner unbelievably, changing direction in their own length, turning so flexibly that they seemed to have no bones.

To a newborn shark the sea lions were an absolute horror. The first one snagged a small shark by the gills, shook it until he broke it, then dropped it to the floor. The second sea lion nabbed another pup and tore its stomach out, pitching the rest away to the pale white crabs that were rising like armies from their tunnels in the mud.

The sea lions were not hungry. They were just playing, amusing themselves. Perhaps, too, deep down, the sea lions had an actual dislike for sharks, for in the end it would almost certainly be a shark that would be the cause of their deaths.

More probably the third and youngest sea lion was just enjoying the chase as he hurtled through and under the waves and, with a whirling arabesque of motion, darted close to Sevengill.

The young male had never killed a shark of this species before. He had toyed with leopard sharks, but they only wiggled as they died. Surely this one would be the same. But still the sea lion hesitated, fanning out his whiskers in investigation. He snorted bubbles at Sevengill's tail, to see what she would do.

In a blur of tail-whipping motion, Sevengill took off. She was thirty feet away before the rush of her momentum died.

One yank of broad chest flippers, and the sea lion caught up. Double-layered hair lay sleek, and bubbles ran the length of his supple, twisting body. More than three times the shark's length he was, and very sure of himself. He did not know that sevengills in general (and this one in particular) are not good creatures to toy with. He should have killed Sevengill or left her alone, because this kind of shark will only run just so far and no farther. After that, things change.

To the left-right-left shot the shark—and then she turned around. What had been a frantic fleeing tail became a set of snapping teeth. Sevengill's face became hideous. Her eyes disappeared down into their sockets, her jaws yanked dislocatingly wide, white teeth stood forward as if on a hinge, and she came back biting *snapsnapsnap!* like wolf traps set off in a row.

The sea lion changed his mind about chasing sevengills, and ducked.

Sevengill zipped through the water where the young sea lion had been, and forgot him almost at once. It is the way of the wild that an emergency once passed is over and done with. Yesterday and tomorrow do not mean much to animals; they deal with the problems of today.

Sevengill left the area slowly, swimming in wide half-circles. This travel pattern was not accidental. She was watching her back trail, in case something should sneak up behind her.

Which was how she happened to meet her mother.

Cruising tiredly along, the eight-foot female looked very much as Sevengill would after the passing of years. Dark. Massive. Graceful. And calm.

Not the slightest hint of recognition passed between the two. The big female shark kept right on swimming, without a glance at the small shark beside her. This was usual for a new mother. She had given her young three gifts—life, the shallows, and a chance to get away.

For two weeks the big female would eat nothing. This not only made mating safe for the smaller male sevengills that might approach her (this being mating time), but also kept the shark pups from being devoured on the spot by their mother.

When the time of truce was over, though, if mother and daughter should happen to meet, it would only be as big and little sharks, and good luck to the swiftest.

Cannibalism may sound gruesome, but it is a natural part of keeping the balance between the sharks and the fish: the eaters and the eaten. Every kind of animal has to have a predator, or the species will multiply too swiftly and eat up all the food supply. If all the mountain lions are killed, the deer will overpopulate and gnaw all the grass to the roots, and afterward starve. But what animal could be the predator of sharks? Very few creatures are fierce enough to try and eat them. But there will never be too many sharks—because sharks prey upon each other.

Sevengill's mother went one way, and Sevengill went the other.

Three weeks later the little shark was swimming underneath the San Mateo Bridge, fourteen miles south of the place where she was born: sticking to the shallows, she had wandered far in search of food.

In the twenty-one days she had been officially alive (not counting two years and eight weeks in the womb), Sevengill had not caught one thing. Normally this would be no problem. Sharks do not need to eat very much. Their bodies have very large livers, accounting for as much as a fourth of their body weight. If Sevengill made a kill, her liver would change the eaten food to a thin, nutritious oil, releasing it slowly to her body. The oil would feed the shark for a surprising length of time, sometimes as much as a month. But Sevengill's birth had been delayed too long. Her liver was dry. Her belly was drawn up, hollow and tight against her spine, and wrinkles showed in her skin.

She had tried many times to catch dinner, but the food was just too quick for her. The truth is, sharks are a little bit clumsy.

Twice the little shark had edged up behind a school of Pacific mackerel, but the fish always seemed to know the difference between a predator just passing through and a predator on the hunt. When Sevengill lunged at them, the mackerel parted like a shower of flung spears and the shark ended up with a mouthful of nothing. Healthy fish are not easy to catch.

The starving shark had also tried for the smallest and most awkward-swimming of three chimaeras, sometimes called rabbit-fish. She sensed that the slow fish would be the easiest to catch. But she had missed even the chimaera again and again, and today she was weaker than when she was born.

The leopard sharks had begun to watch her. Normally these small-mouthed junior predators would never dare to bother a sevengill, even a newborn. They knew too well the power of the husky shark's bite. Sevengills eat leopard sharks as a part of their regular diet. But the slender, shadow-dappled leopard sharks were predators, too, and they knew what weakness was.

One of the leopard sharks was nearly four feet long, a narrow, muscular column of nervous energy. His teeth were small, but they worked very well. He had been studying the movements of Sevengill, half his size, and he detected some flaw, some slight ungracefulness in the way she swam. Something was wrong with her.

The leopard shark moved in closer, testing, brushing her side with his quick-flicking tail, careful to keep out of reach.

Sevengill showed him her teeth, but did not waste her strength in a useless charge. She was too weak with hunger to chase down the leopard shark now.

Her heart beat faster; her stomach got cold. Like all animals, she experienced fear—that jittery feeling as the body's natural stimulant, adrenaline, gets the muscles ready for violence, to fight or get away. She knew very well that the other shark was hunting her, but she kept her movements calm. Appearances are important in the sea. The small shark moved as if nothing were wrong, as if she were the toughest creature in this neighborhood.

The leopard shark was not fooled. He circled, moving faster now, losing his caution. Leopard sharks have eaten weak or wounded sevengills before. He made a quick and tricky run at her, darting near, almost nipping at her short, broad back. When

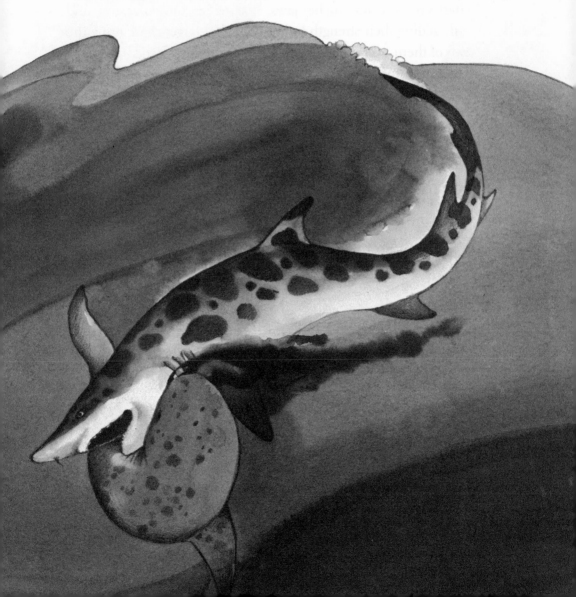

nothing happened, the predator assumed the prey was weak. He repeated the maneuver, getting ready to attack, coming closer, closer . . .

Sevengill waited, and the chill in her stomach turned into heat, and when that over confident gray-black body flicked just near enough—she

For a dist   feet, the charge of a sevengill shark is inv   fastened square on the longer   haking her muscular torso and tai   e. The larger shark flung the two   white bellies flashed and their heads   . The leopard shark was desperate to get awa   ill was also fighting for her life, and her teeth pei   deep into his neck. The coppery taste of blood flooded into her mouth. She had her grip and kept it, and presently the leopard shark was still.

Five years later, on the day when her whole life changed, Sevengill was hunting underneath the Golden Gate Bridge near the entrance to San Francisco Bay.

She was five feet long now, and as pretty as she was going to get. She was built for power and not much for show. Other sharks, like the blue or the great mako, showed sleek lines and spectacular colors. Sevengill was just bulky and strong, and her dominant color was coffee. There were also black spots scattered over her hide, as if a cat had dipped its paws in ink and walked on her. Her stomach was a dead, ugly white. She did not have that tall first dorsal fin on her back, which cuts so spectacularly through the surface and which most people think of when they think of a shark. Her teeth did not even show when she swam, being intended for use and not display. Her single claim to beauty was her eyes, which were gold and black and yet held hints of other hues. In certain lights the flat ovals would look green or even blue.

But if she was no beauty, her senses were astounding. Along her side, in the area where humans are ticklish, ran an opening like a zipper slit. This lateral line was so sensitive that she knew when something swam near, just by the ripples it made. There were also strange pin-sized holes on her snout, which could detect the electricity all life contains, so she could swim past an object and know if it lived; this was handy in hunting. She could also use these ampullae of Lorenzini, as the holes are called, to navigate. Each pinhole held a jellylike substance and a single hair, which sensed the magnetic currents of the earth as does a compass. North was the strongest magnetic attraction; south was away; east and west were right and left. If she chose to leave the bay for a while, she could find her way back home with no trouble.

Her nostrils, small twin caverns on the edges of her snout, were not connected to her breathing apparatus. They were for scent detection only. At the back of the nostrils, wrinkles called Schneiderian folds let the shark sniff out even the most delicate odors.

On the day when her strangest adventure began, Sevengill scented an aroma so strong and enticing, she could not resist investigating it. Cut stingray, rich and sweet; delicate smelt; herring and mackerel powerful as blood—and all together. Its source was a mystery; she knew there had been no killing nearby for a while. If there had been a fight, her lateral line would have felt the vibrations of struggle.

Around the foot of the northernmost pillar of the Golden Gate Bridge she came. At two hundred and fifty feet, the water was pitch black, save for an occasional flash of illumination when the shark's rough body touched plankton with light-emitting photophores, and the microscopic creatures lit up like a twist of soundless lightning. The temperature was a frigid fifty degrees.. Sevengill was quite content.

She was also very curious. The enticing odor came from a most unusual object on the bottom: half a dozen pieces of cut fish, connected. This did not make sense to Sevengill. Fish once bitten apart did not come back together. Not trusting this strangeness, she turned and almost went away. But not quite, because a little leopard shark was zipping back and forth, working up its nerve. It would take the food if the larger shark did not.

Sevengill put her mouth wide around the pile of sweetly odorous fish. Nothing awful happened. She picked the bait up off the bottom, holding it lightly just behind her teeth. Carefully she bit, and changed her course to swim away.

Something poked her in the roof of the mouth. Twice. Three times. With the impact came a fearful pressure which pulled her neck back, interfering with the passage of the water through her gills, cutting down her breath. Sevengill tried to spit out the fish, and the number twelve extra-forge stainless steel shark hook.

Sevengill was torn upward from her place of safety, toward something enormous which growled with ugly motor noises. She fought, but the pressure never eased. The lactic acid of fatigue built up in her muscles. The metal of the boat that was hauling her in confused the ampullae of Lorenzini, those compasslike sensors in her skin, dizzying, disorienting her, as if she had been spun round and round. The silver-mirror surface broke, and something like a white wave reached down and clutched around her. What can sharks know of collector boats and canvas stretchers?

The stench of engine oil was like brutal fingers up her nostrils. In the most terrible moment of her life she was lifted right up out of the water and felt her weight increase by forty times. In the water she weighed three pounds, maybe four, but when gravity crushed down, she gained suddenly to one hundred twenty.

Pale creatures grasped and held her. She tried to bite, to put her teeth into something, but could not. All was confusion and fright as air went hurtfully down her throat, drying her gills, denying her breath. Prods and pliers went into her mouth, holding it open till something went *snick!* and the hook was removed.

With a splash there was coolness, and water around her once more. She breathed, but even this was very strange now, because she was not swimming, nor did she even have to gasp her jaws; yet the water moved by itself through her mouth and throat and gills. On every side was something hard and smooth, and she could not swim away.

Nothing in her life had prepared her for this: for the mysteries of circulating water in a professional shark transport box, or aquariums, or the multifingered beasts called humans.

Sevengill had been caught on a routine collecting trip by San Francisco's Steinhart Aquarium. She would remain at that aquarium for the next two years.

And then her story would intersect with mine.

My First Sharks

2

~~~~~~

When I was little I loved the ocean and dreamed of living there one day. When I became a man—I did!

Not exactly as I had planned, of course; there were no mermaids or underwater houses or giant squids or submarines to play with. But still I had gone to commercial deep-sea diving school, and now I lived in one tiny corner of the ocean for a thousand hours every year.

I was a professional scuba diver for Marine World/Africa USA, an aquarium-zoo then in Redwood City, California. (It would later move up the coast to Vallejo.)

Marine World. Fifty-five acres of carefully tended jungle and carefully maintained ocean. There were lagoons and canals for tour boats to cruise; paths and arenas where people could get close to chimps and cheetahs, elephants, tigers, and lions; an ecology "theater" where people could meet a leopard and learn about worldwide threats to wildlife. There were naturalistic rookeries for sea lions; islands for antelopes, rhinos, flamingos, and monkeys; twenty-foot-long aquariums for the little fish, a half-million-gallon tank for the big ones, and enormous open-air tanks where the dolphins and the killer whales leaped, and people watched and laughed.

It was more than just a business to the folks of the park. Every worker there could have made more money in some other kind of job; the wages were and remain definitely low. But to all of us, Marine World/Africa USA was a celebration of the animal life of land and sea, and I was proud to be a part of it.

Every weekday morning I would suit up in my heavy cloth-and-rubber wet suit and collect my gear from the outside equipment locker. I'd sling a hundred-foot coil of yellow air hose around my shoulder (rather than lug heavy air bottles everywhere, we used the "hookah" arrangement—one end of the hose was connected to a scuba regulator mouthpiece and the other end was a plug for the air compressor outlets we had here and there throughout the park). I would buckle a heavy lead weight belt around my waist to keep the floatable wet suit from tugging me up to the surface. Then I would take down my swim fins and face mask from their pegs on the locker's aged wooden wall—and pick up my scrub brush.

For my work was not as exciting as you might imagine. When I signed on in 1972, the job was described as "like an underwater janitor," and that came pretty close.

What we divers mostly did was swim down into each of the many saltwater tanks and scrub algae off the walls and floors and windows. Algae, the same slime that grows on your fish tank at home, was a real problem for us. The rapidly multiplying single-cell plant would scum over the windows and cloud up the water.

Most ocean displays were cleaned once a week, sometimes more often. A tank left alone would shortly resemble a gigantic algae display. For many reasons this was not desirable, and so we divers scrubbed, and the filters in the tanks sucked the scoured-off algae particles away. Most of the work was repetitious and boring—scrub and scrub and scrub and scrub—but still I was underwater, in the peace and tranquility of the sea.

And if ninety-five percent of my job was hard labor, the rest was pure magic. Dolphins flashed through blue water beside me, and sometimes I'd cling to their backs and fly with them. I got to know killer whales as personalities and spent peaceful hours with giant sea bass big enough to swallow me, swim fins and all.

But one day in the winter of 1978, as I sat at my ancient desk in the grass-thatched dive locker, I was staring out the window and worrying. It was gloomy and chill. The canal-like arm of the lagoon that wound behind our shack looked gray and threatening, reflecting the sky. I could barely make out the neighboring rise with its dark blue buildings—the reef aquarium complex, one of several groups of tanks at Marine World.

That was where the sharks would be arriving, tomorrow, from Steinhart Aquarium.

Sevengill sharks, a species I knew almost nothing about. Would they be even-tempered and calm, or full of violence?

I remembered how nervous I had felt my very first day on the job here, when I had been told to clean the nurse shark tank.

The nurse sharks lived in the reef aquarium complex in a "wall" tank, one of a series of smallish tanks with observation windows along one side of a hallway that curved down from ground level.

As I suited up, I tried to remember everything I knew about

nurse sharks. I had read in books that nurse sharks are harmless bottom-feeders, finding food by shoving their whiskered snouts into the floor of the tropical sea in search of clams or crabs or whatever else they can find. They suck on sand like a baby nursing on a bottle, which is how they got their name. Lazy and sociable, these six-foot sharks are sometimes found in piles around coral right next to the surface, so close to the light they get reddish: sunburned? If left alone, nurse sharks are virtually no threat to a diver at all. Or so the books all said.

But it was different to actually be in the water with a shark as big as I was, just a few feet away, lying on the sand. Gazing at me with its tiny yellow eyes, it crouched on folded fintips as if about to do a pushup. Nurse sharks often perch on their fins, and are said to be able to hop forward quickly from this most unsharklike position. These sharks have a special kind of gill which allows them to both breathe and lie still at the same time. That may not sound like much, but it is an unusual skill for a shark.

Nurse sharks also have jaws that can crunch through clam-shells, or humans with whom they have argued. Captain William Gray of the Miami Seaquarium had a chunk of meat removed from his calf muscle by a nurse shark he was carrying from one tank to another, and people who pulled the tails of even little nurse sharks generally regretted it. I certainly was not going to pull any shark tails. But did the nurse sharks have rules I did not know about? Did they have territories, areas of tank floor, which they would defend?

I would learn the answers to my questions only by being in the tank with them, so I slipped quietly into the warm water and prepared to do my job.

To scrub the walls, I hung from a gray suction cup which I

could move from place to place. Five inches across, the cup was the kind glass-movers use, a rubber disk inside a metal "teacup." Putting the rubber disk next to the wall, I depressed a little lever, and *glom:* the cup made a vacuum and sucked on. It was natural and easy to hang with all my weight suspended, scrubbing with one arm and gripping the cup with the other, both feet braced on the wall.

The water was heated to a comfortable eighty degrees and was very clear at first. When the nurse sharks did nothing, only crouched on the floor underneath me, I relaxed and scrubbed maroon and purple algae off the wall. The water swirled with purple fog as the inch-thick mats of vegetation lifted. It was fun. I felt like Tarzan, all my weight suspended from one hand, clinging to the wall.

Then the suction cup slipped. My heavy weight belt tugged me down. I landed on my rear end. Something wriggled violently underneath me. *I was sitting on the nurse shark's head!* As I struggled frantically to get up, I remember quite distinctly thinking: If I get bit back there, I won't even be able to show off the scars.

But the nurse shark only shrugged me off and lumbered a few feet away to a more peaceful section of the tank. I was very glad the shark had not lived up to its reputation—as a bottom-feeder.

It was fun now, on this cold winter day of 1978, to look back and remember. And despite my nervousness about the arriving sevengills, in some ways I was glad Marine World was getting them. They were slated for the big reef aquarium tank, on the other side of the hallway from the wall tanks. That wonderful tank deserved the sense of menace and completeness that only

sharks can bring. There was also another and more practical purpose for adding the sharks—a purpose we learned about only through a tragedy.

My favorite underwater place, "the reef" was huge, one of the largest aquarium tanks in the world. Twenty feet deep, fifty feet wide, eighty feet long, the oval-shaped tank held five hundred thousand gallons of filtered seawater and several artificial reefs made of natural-looking fiberglass. Thirty-two observation windows looked out on the hallway that spiraled down halfway around the tank. Overhead, the tank was partially roofed with a vast sheet of rubberized canvas to shade the inhabitants.

The reeftank was like a little ocean, not sterile or controlled like some aquarium exhibits, with only one or two species of animals guaranteed not to fight. No, the reeftank almost always held a mix of fish, predators and prey. It was not tame; it was the wild. Anything that could happen out in the ocean could happen here.

Now the reeftank was cold, unheated, like our coastal waters; but once it had been tropical, eighty degrees, a paradise. But it had no sharks.

Then the reeftank's water had been Australian blue, and that is a compliment. There is no finer, clearer water in the world—blue-white, and with animals more beautiful and varied than even Walt Disney's imagination could invent.

Tarpon like quicksilver memories, motionless one instant, somewhere else the next. Alligator gar from the still, brown lakes of Texas, which never seemed to move. Damselfish, which never stopped moving, six-inch chunks of fury that would mercilessly peck a diver till he or she had to leave the neighborhood. Parrot fish with hard-fused teeth to grind up coral. Surgeonfish, which carried pieces of sharp cartilage like concealed knives behind their ears. But no sharks.

Giant sea bass, ten feet long and a quarter of a ton apiece, gray-green, that changed color and disappeared if they got nervous, which was not often. When they got angry they boomed, a sound so loud we divers could feel it in our bodies. If they got really mad, I heard, they could stab with spikes like switchblades on their back. Groupers or gropers, jewfish or junefish, as the sea bass were variously called, changed their sex when they got old. They started life as females, were impregnated and bore young, and then switched sex, becoming male for the rest of their lives.

Every time we dived in that tank, there was something new to see. Sturgeon like sharks but without tempers or teeth, mild-mannered living vacuum cleaners of the floor. Puffer fish like lengths of white sausage until they got scared, when they could puff up like spiky basketballs. Wrasse, who would swim into the mouths of the giant groupers unharmed. The three-inch rainbow-colored wrasse are among the most valuable members of an underwater community, eating the parasites off any fish who cares to hold still for the service. In the wild, fish will line right up, waiting their turn at the wrasse cleaning station.

But there were no sharks in paradise, and that was terribly important, because one day the reef began to die.

An angelfish fell trembling to the bottom of the tank. I picked up the gorgeous thing, sunspot yellow fringed with iridescent blue, neon colors just beginning to fade. I felt it shiver, felt its life go out in my hands.

At first there were only two or three pale stomachs of dead fish shining up at us from the bottom of the tank. Then there were a dozen. Then a hundred.

The surgeonfish died violently, stabbing with their little knives against an invisible enemy they could not fight. The alligator gar passed on with the dignity of ages, and the damselfish went still. A moray eel who had bitten my finger for holding him too long became nothing but a length of limp brown jelly, muscles gone flaccid in death.

We never really found out what killed the reef. But if it was disease, sharks might have stopped it. In the wild, sharks halt fish epidemics by eating the sick fish first. Because they are immune to most forms of disease, sharks can eat sick fish without catching the illness themselves. This stops the spread of disease, and keeps the ocean healthy.

But there were no sharks in the reeftank. The tarpon died and the sturgeon died and the cleaning wrasse died: two thousand fish in three weeks. Divers who were normally as playful as otters now sat and stared at nothing in between dives with the hateful plastic trash bags, body bags for fish we had come to know as individuals. The reef was perhaps the single most beautiful object in our lives, like a diamond, only better because it was alive. Now it was dying before our eyes, and we were helpless to make the killing stop. We just pulled the small finned corpses out and dissected them or threw them away.

Once I bagged and removed three hundred fish by myself, counting them as numbers so I would not really think about what was happening, piling up bag after bag. Suddenly I could not do it anymore. I plunged up out of the water and went someplace and hid for a while, as though by running away I could make the dying not be true.

At last even the giant sea bass left their cave in the reef and came out in the open in daytime, which was not usual for them.

The enormous fish lay head to head in the sunlight for an hour. Then they separated. It was as if they had been saying good-bye. They swam to different corners of the reef and lay still. Slowly the green-and-granite coloration faded. When their bodies were a pale and lifeless gray, we dragged them out with ropes.

The heaters were turned off, because the fish were gone.

But now, in 1978, the reef before me was full of fish once again, this time from our own California coastline. It did not hold the technicolor glory of the tropics anymore, and the water was more often cloudy with algae, but it had its own beauty, quiet, less spectacular, but real. Green-and-white kelp bass, massive-bodied sheepheads of crimson and black, garibaldi like sparks of orange fire. Striped bass and yellowtail and big sea turtles. There were some small sharks in the reef now too, three- to five-foot leopard sharks, two- to three-foot spiny dogs, eighteen-inch horn sharks which laid eggs called mermaid purses—but nothing big. Nothing like sevengills.

On the canal outside my dive shack window, the water's dark surface swirled as a gust of wind suddenly whooshed by. Black clouds were already piled high as mountains, and still they continued to build. There would be a lot of rain tomorrow when the sevengill sharks arrived.

Behind me I heard the rusty heater humming as it warmed the two-room dive shack. My hands were still cold from the afternoon dive, and I turned toward the friendly glow. But as I leaned close to the red-hot coils, I shivered suddenly, and not from cold. I was remembering another glowing wire, an incandescent filament in a dying floodlight, set up in an aquarium hallway. It had happened years ago at three o'clock in the morning on a night I spent in the water with a great white shark.

*　　*　　*

You can imagine how I felt earlier that night when I was called at home and told that a net-caught white shark was being brought to Marine World. As head diver, I was naturally expected to help with the shark, meaning to get into the water with it. San Francisco's world-renowned Steinhart Aquarium had had the shark first, but their largest tank was not yet completed, and they had no enclosure big enough to house this diver's nightmare.

The ride to Marine World was the most terrifying forty minutes of my life. My stomach felt squeezed and kneaded by invisible fingers. The sky was black and seemed to be closing over my head. I envisioned every horrific possibility, remembered every shark attack scene I had ever read about or seen at the movies, imagined the teeth like knives, closing through my body. Maybe the shark would bite my swim fins off, with my feet still in them. I wished I were a kid again so I could go back to bed and forget the whole thing.

The animal waiting for me was small, as white sharks go, seven feet six inches, three hundred fifty pounds, but that gave me no comfort. The worst single shark attack in history, the real-life incident on which the book and movie *Jaws* were based, had involved a white shark only six inches longer. That had happened in 1916 at Matawan Creek, New Jersey. In a freak occurrence an eight-foot white shark had swum up a river and gotten trapped. Perhaps through fear or because it was denied its natural food, the white shark killed four people and wounded a fifth before it was caught and positively identified by the human remains in its stomach. "Our" shark from Steinhart was just about that size. What if it panicked, or got angry, thinking we were trying to hurt it?

All too quickly the distance passed, and I pulled up at the back gate of Marine World/Africa USA.

The guard shack was brightly lit, but when I'd run past the giraffe and elephant barns, past the shining eyes of wolves, and got to the divers' shower room, I had to dress in the dark. Redwood City was having some minor electrical supply problems that summer. That was okay, though. I was the largest diver and could pick out my wet suit by its weight. I stripped and climbed into the sleeveless "farmer johns," not bothering with the jacket this warm summer night. I was anxious to get into the water with the shark and not have to think about it anymore. When I was halfway suited up, the electricity came back on, which was a relief.

With swim fins and scuba gear and air hose on, I stood at the darkened staircase leading down to the entryway into the reef aquarium tank. The square of water below me *glowed*—a ghastly writhing green. It was only because floodlights had been set up to shine into the tank from the windowed hallway below, but knowing that did not help. To me right then, the wavering green water looked like the doorway to hell.

But, I reminded myself, the white shark from Steinhart was an animal in trouble. She had just suffered what had to be the most terrible day in her life. Half-strangled in fishermen's nets, towed behind a boat with a heavy fishhook through her jaw, and finally jounced around in a water-filled box on the back of a truck, she would be groggy, dazed, barely conscious. If left alone in our tank, she would almost certainly die.

But if the divers "walked" her, which in this case meant swimming her around the big reeftank, this would push water down her throat, making her breathe until she could do it on her own:

artificial respiration for a shark. Huh! I wasn't going to give her mouth-to-mouth!

Adjusting my weight belt, and splashing my fintip in the water at the foot of the stairs, I tried to think if there was anything else I needed. Oh, yes, definitely—a shark stick—a two-foot length of inch-thick stainless steel (taken from a gate broken by a killer whale's bite) with a blue bicycle-handle grip glued to one end. I stuck one loosely under the loop of my belt and practiced pulling it out like a sword. I liked that part. I was not sure exactly what I would do with the stick against an excited white shark, but it was solid and comforting next to my stomach.

I was supposed to take over from the diver who was presently in the tank. I ducked down into the water and felt the surface close over my head. Out into the eerie green light I swam. My arms and legs felt very long, like bait. I pulled my arms in close and my legs together, swimming with just my hands and fins. I considered holding the shark stick in my hand but was afraid I would be laughed at, so I kept it tucked behind the quick-release buckle of my weight belt.

Where were they? All I could see was one of our artificial reefs, big as a hill, and directly before me a large school of kelp bass. Suddenly they scattered in all directions as something huge burst through them!

I pulled out the shark stick so quick my belt almost fell off. But it was only old Chopper, our giant loggerhead, five hundred pounds of frantic-swimming sea turtle, hustling away from one of the very few predators who could give her trouble. Even an inch-thick armored shell is insufficient protection against a bite like the blow of an axe.

Then I saw them: the man and the great white shark. The human, Dave Worcester, a killer-whale trainer, was powerfully built, with a weight-lifter's arms and shoulders. But he did not loom large above the beast he held.

The white shark was beautiful. I had not been prepared for that. The dead animals I had seen photographed on the beach or fishermen's boats had been flattened by gravity, crushed by their own weight. Dead, the animals had seemed distorted, squashed, ugly. But alive and moving, the female white shark was graceful, magnificent, a work of living art.

Everything about her seemed designed to fit together in one smoothly functioning unit: from conical snout-tip to cavernous chest to crescentic half-moon tail. She was structured for power and torrents of speed, built for the charge and the kill. Her mouth was very nearly as wide as the width of her torso. One glance at the terrible notch-edged white teeth was enough to know she would be fierce and unsympathetic when aroused. The ultimate predator among fish, the great white fights the giant mammals of the sea, like Steller's sea lions, bigger than swimming grizzly bears. No small-mouthed shark could thin those herds, I thought as I swung wide around her forest of teeth.

Approaching from the back, I tapped the diver on the shoulder. His head yanked around and his eyes bulged white behind the mask. Then he realized it was just his replacement and raised his hand in the thumb-and-circled-forefinger okay sign. He flippered away to go get some rest, leaving me alone with the shark. I would not have objected if he had wanted to stay.

Feeling very unprepared for this, I put my hands on the shark's broad, rough back. The muscles underneath felt like the columns that hold up buildings. Her skin was smooth as I slid one bare hand back to grip her dorsal fin, but when I pushed the other hand forward to guide her head, the skin teeth, or denticles, dug into my fingertips. No wonder sharkskin was once used for the handles of swords. That grip was not going to slip.

I pushed her head with one hand and pulled her black-fringed dorsal with the other, and the white shark swam. Slowly. It was hard work for me, like pushing a lawn mower uphill through weeds. The shark was heavy and wanted to sink. She moved with an appearance of effort, as if she was almost asleep, groggy with oxygen deprivation. She must not be getting enough water down her throat and over her gills to let her breathe properly. I swam faster, hauling her heavily along, laboring to increase the flow of water through her open mouth. It seemed to help. She swam—slowly—but she was definitely moving on her own, making small independent motions, steering us in different directions.

For a long time nothing much happened. The situation began to seem unreal, as though I were pushing a surfboard or a sandpaper-covered model of a shark. I leaned forward to look at her face.

Her lower jaw flexed in a half-chewing motion as though testing the equipment—those serrate-edged teeth which could slip so easily into flesh. Her wide-slatted leathery gill covers, five on a side, flared out and contracted, partially under her muscular control. As I leaned forward I could also see one of her eyes. White shark's eyes are said to be expressionlessly black. Hers were. But there was also a faint mist of blue, a chill and covering color, over the black eyeball. It was the eye Death would have, if Death were a fish. The eye looked back and saw me. I returned to my position and did not look front again.

The trouble with doing anything dangerous is that after a while it becomes routine. As the night wore on and the divers and trainers took turns with the white shark, we became almost casual about it. Fatigue set in, wearying the muscles, clouding the judgment.

After a while it became too much trouble to take the shark sticks in with us. The other guys left them behind altogether. I kept bringing mine along, but when it slipped out of my belt and wibble-wobbled in a glittering circle down to the floor, I didn't want to set the shark down and go get it. Besides, the stainless steel bar was heavy, easily weighing six or seven pounds, which is quite a bit when you are swimming. I told myself I would go get it later, and then forgot all about it.

Until three o'clock in the morning, when Redwood City had another power failure. One moment I was swimming the shark into a pool of white light, the next the floodlights flickered, darkened to a red glow, and went out.

I could see nothing.

Worse, the darkness triggered something in the animal I held. Perhaps she thought she was returning to the lightless deep. I felt the different, stronger rhythm waking in her muscles, and heard the meshing click of teeth, like fitted instruments. *Shclick. Shclick.* I knew it was her teeth. My hand was on the top of her head, and I felt the impact as her jaws came together.

"Don't get excited," I thought to the shark. "Just relax. Wait till the lights come back on."

Black water rushed past my face as the shark increased her speed. The crescent tail banged against my shins. I lifted my legs and the shark towed me, easily, in the vastness of her returning strength. Then, with a twist of her body that numbed my gripping hands, she broke away.

I fumbled at my weight-belt buckle, but the shark stick was not there. I was weaponless and blind, alone in the water with a great

white shark, symbol of all that is savage: *Carcharodon carcharias*, man-eater, white death, *Jaws*. There was only one thing to do, and I did it.

I hid.

Sharks are attracted to motion, so I would hide by holding still on the bottom. Releasing my air in a short whoosh of bubbles, I sank, hoping I would not land on a night-swimming green moray eel. My fintips touched the floor. My back bumped something rough. An instant's shock, and then I remembered the fiberglass reef.

I held absolutely still, trying not to breathe. Only my eyes moved behind the mask.

Denied sight, my other senses struggled harder. I could smell the saltwater sloshing in the nosepiece of my mask, feel the ridging bite of fiberglass in the reef against my back. And then I heard it.

The Stillness. I had read that "white sharks bring the stillness," but I never really knew what that meant. Until now. A peculiar deathlike quality of silence hung throughout the tank. I had not realized it till this instant, but normally there is a very faint undercurrent of motion noise as the fish swim about their business. Now, nothing. Every creature in that tank was doing exactly what I was doing. We all held absolutely still so as not to attract the attention of a nervous super predator. We waited.

There was moonlight, and gradually sight returned. As my eyes adjusted, close-up details showed first: the gills and spines of a kelp bass, breathing, then its schoolmates, hanging in the water in a formation, imitating the pattern of the long-bladed seaweed in which they would hide in the wild.

Then I saw the ghostly outline: the white shark, moving fast.

But she was not attacking. She hunted breath, not food. She was trying to shake off the grogginess of oxygen deprivation the only way she knew: by swimming forward fast. Maybe she thought she was going home.

She must have seen the wall, but she had no way to understand it. In the wild a wall of white could be moonlight, or a school of shining fish or squid, which would part, offering no obstruction to a moving great white shark. She could not know about concrete. She accelerated, moving faster and faster, and there was nothing I could do.

With a thudding impact so loud the sound was heard outside the tank, the white shark rammed headfirst into the wall. The concussion shook her body. She fell, shuddering, to the floor.

And the moonlight was her grave.

Even now, sitting in my dive locker on a wintry day long after, I felt again the wonderment at her beauty and strength, and a mixed sense of sadness and relief that she had died. Part of me had wanted very badly for her to live, so people could come and see her for what she was, a glorious big fish. She was not the bloodthirsty monster she was made to look like in the movies. But another part of me was relieved that she had died. What would it have been like to work in the reeftank with a large and possibly dangerous shark swimming around behind me?

Starting tomorrow, I would find out.

Tomorrow the sevengill sharks were arriving. One of them had something in common with me, for she also had spent a night in the water with a great white shark.

It had happened two years earlier. Steinhart Aquarium had obtained another great white: a hook-caught male, six feet long, still bleeding slightly at the jaw. This time Steinhart did not need to bring it to our park; their biggest tank, a beautiful doughnut-shaped glass-walled exhibit called the Roundabout, was now complete, and hopes were high.

Once more, divers pushed a white shark forward, helping it to breathe. But this time there was another big inhabitant in the tank: a large brown sevengill shark, a female, five feet long and only there a couple of months herself. She appeared to be curious about the slow-swimming white. Cruising in alongside the bigger animal, the sevengill moved her tail oddly, lashing it out but not quite allowing it to touch. This maneuver would bounce water back from the investigated object, so the sevengill's sensitive lateral line could guess how tough and healthy the white shark was by the way the ripples returned to her. Apparently it told her what she wanted to know.

Because the smaller shark lunged in between the divers and fastened her jaws on the neck of the ocean's fiercest predator. The sevengill's body shook back and forth and she tore out a section of the white shark's throat. Swallowing that, she commenced to eat the white shark alive. Understandably, the divers did not interfere with her.

Now, two years later, the brown shark with black spots and golden eyes had grown larger. And starting tomorrow, she would be swimming in the waters of Marine World/Africa USA.

It occurred to me that my own small adventure with a white shark was something I would never forget: a memory to treasure and tell for the rest of my days.

But to the shark that I would shortly know as Sevengill, the great white shark was just another wounded fish to eat.

The Sevengills Arrive

3

~~~~~~

Rain! Gray, hard-driven rain, roaring, pouring torrents of it, rain to make you cover your mouth if you wanted one unhindered breath, rain so fierce and flooding that only a diver like me in a snug rubber wet suit could be truly comfortable outside—that was the rain on the day the sevengill sharks arrived at Marine World/Africa USA.

Running across the bridge toward the dolphin show stadium, behind which the sharks would soon be unloaded, I was filled with excitement. Adventure waited just ahead; we were getting *sharks* today! No mild-natured nurse sharks or timorous little leopards—sevengills! Hunters! No more for us would sharks be mere glimpsed shadows in the sea, or monsters lurching across the movie screen. Now they would be real and alive and with us every day, every time we divers went into the reef.

There it was. Steinhart's aquarium truck loomed suddenly, like a hillside in the rain.

With a roar the door at the back opened up, disappearing onto rollers in the ceiling. Inside, light glowed behind a container like a large white open coffin. A gray-haired man in a black rain slicker stood there—Dave Powell, the curator of fishes at Steinhart Aquarium at that time. He nodded as I clambered aboard, eager to see what was inside the box.

Bubbles. A million billion coldly boiling bubbles.

"Aeration," said Curator Powell, flipping a switch so that the bubbles subsided. "It oxygenates the water, keeps the sharks happy on the trip."

He plunged his arms into the water, came up with something that wriggled and fought. He handed it to me. It was a baby shark.

"Watch your fingers," Curator Powell said. "Sevengills, you know."

The shark in my tight-gripping hands was less than three feet long, but it wriggled like a wrestler's leg. The tail fin braced against my forearm and white teeth reached back, straining to bite. A leopard shark in this situation would have been whipping and hitching side to side, trying to swim, desperate to get away. This little sevengill wanted to fight. The teeth on the top jaw were like ivory fishhooks; the lower teeth looked like sections of saw.

Getting down from the truck without using my hands was an exercise in caution. Squatting down to the edge of the truck floor, I sat, scooted off, fell a long split second to land in an exaggerated crouch. My hands were way out in front of me.

"We'll need a stretcher for the bigger ones," I heard Dave Powell say behind me as I hurried along the walkway beside the dolphin show bleachers, toward the back of the adjoining reeftank. Dolphins bobbed up at once in their pool on the right, smiling their permanent smiles in the rain, curious about what was going on. I said hello politely, as one does to animals at Marine World, but did not take my eyes off what I carried. I stepped down onto the dolphin stage, and then behind the painted backdrop, where visitors seldom go.

Beyond the dolphin grotto was the reef aquarium tank, its surface continually smashed by the rain. The water droplets hit so hard they seemed to bounce. The boundaries between air and water and land seemed blurry and uncertain.

I pitched the little shark out and down. With a slap and a splash it disappeared. No ominous triangular fin cut the surface. It seemed unfair that this kind of shark lacks that tall first dorsal fin on the back—less warning somehow.

" 'Scuse us!" somebody said, and I got out of the way of a diver and the next shark, which was a little larger than the one I had transported.

The sharks we were getting today were young, ranging in size from two to six and a half feet long. The average shark in the ocean is only about four feet fully grown, with eighty-two percent of all species never exceeding six and a half feet at maturity. Our sevengills might grow to a girthy nine feet, as large or larger than anything we were likely to meet in the wild.

The smaller sharks we dropped in from the top as I had done; the five-foot fall to the water was no problem for them. But the heavier ones might be hurt if allowed to belly-flop down. Sharks have no ribs to protect their insides, and we feared the sudden impact on the water's top might rupture some delicate internal organs.

Which was why I was soon standing nervously in waist-deep

water in the flume, a shallow rectangular tank connected to the reef like a chute. Before me was a set of redwood stairs climbing out of the water; behind me was the open doorway to the reef.

The larger sevengills would be brought to the reeftank on stretchers, like the ones in hospitals, only bigger and with more canvas so they could wrap around the animal. Each stretcher would be lowered onto the slanting steps, at the foot of which I waited. One side of the short staircase was open, so I could walk alongside the stairs if necessary. I was supposed to separate the stretcher poles, grab hold of the shark, guide it across the flume, and push it through the reef entryway.

Down the stairs, across the flume, out into the reeftank—it worked very well at first. The bigger sharks stayed quiet, almost not struggling at all. This was not so tough, I thought. No problem.

Bubbles rose from the floor beside me. A safety diver was lying there with a length of sawed-off broomstick. His name was Reid Dennis, and his task was to turn away any shark who tried to come back into the flume. I was glad he was there. I could not see the animals after I pushed them out the entryway, and it was scary to let go of an animal that might turn around and start fighting. Some people who had been attacked by sharks said the actual bite did not hurt, that some chemical on shark teeth numbed the wound. Other victims said it hurt like crazy. I did not want to find out for sure.

Now as I waited anxiously for the last and largest, number thirteen, the female who had killed the great white shark, I wondered about these new arrivals.

Sevengills. Nobody knew much about them. The books all said about the same thing: "The sevengill shark, *Notorynchus maculatus* (lately N. *cepedianus*), also called broadhead, is considered to be aggressive and dangerous. It has been found with human remains in its stomach, and is known to have attacked divers in aquariums."

I did not know what the "human remains" part meant. There is a big difference between a swimmer eaten alive and a piece of some drowned person scavenged off the bottom of the bay. As for the aquarium attack part, I knew that had happened at least once.

A diver named Norval Greene had been force-feeding a small (sixteen-pound) sevengill, pushing half a mackerel down its throat. He was trying to save the shark's life, but it did not understand. It broke away from him, shot back, and tore into the diver's upraised forearm, which was protecting his face. The sevengill shook violently, removing a substantial chunk of Greene's forearm. The shark did not eat what it had taken, but spat out the piece of meat, which was dip-netted from the water and surgically reattached to the diver. Greene recovered after a month in the hospital, but the shark died. Dissection revealed a broken jaw, which might have happened in the feeding and could well have been the reason for the attack.

Fishermen recommended that you watch your fingers around sevengills, crossbay swimmers reported being approached by the heavy-bodied brown-and-black sharks, and there was some ugly speculation that maybe the convict who had disappeared from the old prison hellhole on Alcatraz Island had not really escaped at all, but had only traded his life sentence for a swift execution in San Francisco Bay.

Aside from this, there was a very large silence on the subject of the sevengill shark.

"Comin' at you!" I heard, and looked up. Two men walked

backward through the sheets of rain, each carrying the ends of a stretcher's bending poles. Underneath, I saw the bulging canvas move: once to the right side, once to the left, as if its occupant were testing the strength of its confines. Even through the coarse weave of canvas I could see the bulge of heavy jaw.

I scrambled up the redwood steps. With several people helping, we lugged the shark, still in the stretcher, head downward on the sloping stairs.

Once back down the stairs in the water I gingerly pulled one end of the stretcher pole. A large flat eye looked up at me. I put the stretcher canvas back. I wanted to think about this some more.

"Can I get a picture?"

It was the photographer.

Normally I do not like to be photographed. But with a shark in my arms no one would be looking at me anyway, and besides, what a nice scrapbook shot—oh, this is me and the shark, I could say, deepening my voice just a little.

"Sure, go ahead," I said, and got ready to move. Now would be a tricky moment, for at the first hint of release, some restrained animals explode into motion. I peeled back the canvas and lunged forward, locking forearms and elbows onto the top of the shark. My fingers clutched onto the skin, but carefully. I had held animals still before, and there is a definite art to it. The trick is not to squeeze in, but around, to make a ring of control. Unless the animal tries to move, it should not really feel pressure, being aware of the holder mainly as warmth, although the person may be shaking with exertion. As I was now. But the photographer was not satisfied.

"Um, actually I just wanted the shark—could you move back out of the way, please?"

Oh. All right. I did as I was asked, stepping away from the shark on the steps, releasing my grip from the animal's uncovered back. It was a mistake.

The flashbulb exploded, and everything changed. In the green glare after the blinding white light, I saw the shark bend double, as if she were trying to swim up the stairs. The only safe place to be was right on her back, and I put half of me there just as quick as I could. As chin and elbows scraped muscle and sandpaper hide, I shouted to the men at the top of the stairs.

"Let loose her tail!" I yelled, having a pretty good idea what was about to happen. The top stretcher poles were still crossed, restraining the tail of the shark. The shark only wanted the water, and I was anxious she should have it.

"What? What?" came down from above, but I need not have worried. Before the others could understand and spread the stretcher poles, the shark took care of that detail herself. Straightening her body with astonishing speed, she flung me and her backward, slamming my head against the concrete flume wall, shaking herself quite free of the stretcher. I lost my footing and went under: saw bubbles, green water, and the dark thing I held. There was no time to be afraid; I was too busy. Saltwater shot up my nose and I choked, but retained just enough sense to hang on. Let loose of a terrified shark in close quarters?

I felt concrete underneath my feet, felt the steps behind me now. I got my balance and carefully stood, sneezed violently, and shoved the shark out of the flume. I pushed her as if moving a couch, and she shot out into the reeftank beyond.

The next instant was so *quiet*. One moment the shark had filled my whole existence; the next I was staring at the empty entryway. She could easily have bitten me right then, I thought, if she had turned around. But she hadn't. It was over!

I raised my arms and hollered, but the yell turned into a screech like that of an injured pterodactyl. Something glommed onto my leg! Frantically I kicked with what I hoped was not a stub of knee. I tried to scramble backward for the steps, but something dark rose up in front of me. I hauled back my fist to punch just as hard as I possibly—

The black object came into focus. It was diver Reid Dennis's black wet-suit hood, keeping R.D. warm while he was underwater. His diver's mask was askew and half-filled with water; the regulator mouthpiece he had been breathing from hung by one plastic toothgrip. *Ptoo*, he spit it out like some foreign object. His blue eyes were blurred. I had been kicking the man who had been down below all along, guarding my legs.

"I jus' wanted you to move back a li'l bit, was all," said the normally crisp-dictioned diver.

The storm was drizzling out. Patches of pale light appeared. I was apologizing to Reid for about the eighth time and feeling glad the whole thing was over, when we heard the sound of running footsteps.

It was a messenger, panting, up from the windowed hallway below.

"One of your sharks is in trouble," he said.

In a wavering beam of sunlight lay a middle-sized sevengill, belly-up, white stomach almost gleaming against dark algae on the floor. Long clasper fins used in mating identified it as a male. He looked dead, like something on ice in a fish store. But as we swam nearer, breathing through our regulators and yellow "hookah" air lines, we could see that the four-and-a-half-foot shark was breathing, too, moving his jaws, faintly pulling in a little bit of water, trying to remain alive.

I turned the husky animal over, which made him look better already. His two-tone color pattern gave him double defensive camouflage; from above, his dark back would be hard to spot against the ocean floor; from underneath the white belly would get lost in the gleam of the surface.

From the corner of my eye I saw the biggest sevengill, who just happened to be swimming by. I remembered what she had done to the hook-wounded great white. Not again, I thought.

Then I had a bright idea. Instead of slowly swimming around and around with the shark in my arms, maybe I could revive the animal by giving it one huge chestful of water all at once.

Standing on the bottom, I picked up the shark. It was the size of a German shepherd or a small but well-fed wolf. Lifting him was easy, since he weighed almost nothing in the water. I raised him to arms' length over my head and threw him.

It worked spectacularly. The water burst down his throat like a current of electricity, jolting him awake. Faster than I'd thought a shark could move, the chunky creature flashed away. Left, right, left he picked up speed.

He turned around and came back at the level of my face, jaws snapping.

Everything seemed to happen in slow motion. I saw the pale underside of his snout lift and the lower jaw come forward, saw the mouth open up incredibly wide, wide as the width of the shark. I saw white teeth and the slatted vents of gills, looked down the throat to the white buccal cavity before the twist of stomach, saw what the doomed fish sees. Then the teeth slammed together again and again, *whunk whunk whunk*, a sound like wolf traps snapping, and every time I thought they were biting me.

Then I was flat on my back on the floor and the shark kept

right on going, still biting blind. He acted as if he had gone insane, a berserker shark, scattering a cloud of kelp bass, almost ramming into the big reef cave, hurtling in a circle up to the fiberglass and metal aeration trough which circled the top of the tank. Incredibly he *bit* the aeration trough, raking his teeth along it, leaving scratches in the paint.

"That was crazy, junior," I thought when my heart rate subsided, and thus the shark Crazy Junior was named.

I stood up again and noticed the big female was still in the neighborhood, cruising on by without the slightest visible trace of fear. She swam slowly, calmly, with a minimum of effort. She seemed bigger in her natural element, but even without the magnification of liquid she was longer in the water than I was tall on land. Her head looked as wide as a child's school desk, and at each side of her jaw was a bulge of extra skin to accommodate the mass of muscle there and allow room for the jaws to open dislocatingly wide, as the smaller shark's mouth had done.

Something thumped into my back and this time it wasn't any diver. *Quickripscratch* I felt rough skin and cloth mesh and disengage. I spun and Crazy Junior was dashing off again. Had it been an accident? He had only bumped, not bitten. Was he as anxious to part company with me as I was with him? Was it a warning, a buildup to something more, or just a coincidence?

With an effort I slowed my breathing. It was all I could do to maintain self-control. I decided I had had about enough sharks for one day. Drawing a finger across my throat, I signaled to the other diver my intention to go home. He nodded, and we left, watching each other's backs all the way.

Tomorrow would be better, I told myself.

But it was not.

Eye to Eye with Sevengill

4

The morning after the sharks arrived, the reeftank windows needed to be cleaned. Even in the middle of winter, when colder temperatures slowed the growth of algae, the single-celled plant multiplied too fast to be ignored. Left alone, the windows would soon disappear beneath a wave of vegetable slime, and the aquarium would look like one big algae display.

Lindy Mitchell-Cook, my diving partner for the morning, and I hunted up our nylon-bristle window brushes and headed for the reef.

For myself, I was in no great hurry to go back in with the sharks. The events of yesterday were still fresh in my mind: the explosion of energy when the big female sevengill fought in the flume, the sound of Crazy Junior's jaws slamming together, the ugly instant when I thought a shark was biting my leg. I was willing to let the sharks alone for a while, like maybe two or three years.

Lindy Mitchell-Cook is one of my favorite people in the world. She was the first female professional diver I ever worked with, and I had wondered at first if she could do her share of the underwater chores. She did. My greater body weight gave me an advantage on the wire-brush floor-scrubbing, but she developed a complicated kick-and-scrub method with a light nylon brush on the walls that I could not duplicate. On the floor I did twice as much as she could; on the walls she left me in a cloud of scrubbed-off algae. It evened out.

Slender but well-muscled, Lindy could be relied upon in any emergency, although always in her own special way. I remember she had worn garden gloves when her turn came to push the great white shark. It looked funny, as if she were going to go manure some roses. Besides, the water was warm, what was the point? Or so I thought, until my fingers lost skin, turning red as their natural callus caps rubbed away from gripping the shark's rough hide. It happened gradually. I did not notice the skin scraping off until it was too late. Without that layer of protective callus, dead skin, the fingers were terrifically sensitive. When I went home next morning, my wife, Jeannie, handed me a glass of chilled orange juice, and the coldness burned like frozen fire. For the next few days, touching anything was an unpleasant surprise. Lindy's gloves did not seem quite so silly anymore.

She did not have her gloves on today, I noticed, as we got ready to go into the reef. But then we did not plan to touch any sharks.

I was having difficulty working up any spit. Divers need to spit in their masks before diving. It sounds offensive, but it really is not; something in the saliva remains invisibly after rinsing, preventing the lens from fogging up. Today, however, I seemed to be a little short on antifog material. Also, my legs had developed a mysterious tendency to wobble, my forehead was beaded with cold sweat, and my stomach seemed to belong to somebody else.

I looked over at Lindy. I would not have minded if she had seemed a little worried. Then I could have said something reassuring, like that the sharks would probably be scared of us at first and stay away, being nervous around humans the way most animals are.

But Lindy only hummed a little tune as she tucked her long brown hair under the wet-suit hood. Her blue eyes were cheerful, and her face expressed general happiness, just looking for a chance to break out in a smile. Exasperating woman. Didn't she realize we were about to go swimming with the monsters of the deep?

"Mmghmf?" I asked, my enunciation somewhat hampered by the regulator in my mouth. Lindy, understanding, nodded back: yes, she was ready. We clambered down the redwood steps into the shallow water of the flume. I squatted down, wanting to get used to the water here, rather than plunging blindly out into the reef.

I heard a soft sucking pop as the water closed over my head. There was always some shock of element exchange when I left the world of dryness and air, and my mind ceased to function for a second. Then I grew accustomed to the coolness, to the peace and silence. Water being constant all around, I did not feel wet very long, and despite the thirty-pound weight belt and scuba gear, I felt almost weightless, able to fly. I heard the roar of bubbles from our mouthpiece exhausts; down here, the only air was what we brought along.

Peeking cautiously out the reef entryway, I searched for unfriendly traffic. Nothing approached along our level. But fifteen feet below us, in the chill, clear water, a thick-bodied shape cruised slowly by.

We waited until the shark had passed, then took one giant step forward, breathing out our air.

Like a slow-motion fall off a cliff, we sank toward the floor and the windows below. I tried to stabilize, paddling with my hands so as to stay upright. For some reason it seemed important to remain vertical, in human posture, as the weight belt tugged me down.

Down into nightmare. As my fintips folded under my feet and my heels hit the bottom, I crowded right back to the wall. From the right and the left the sharks were coming at us.

With my scrub brush I thumped the nearest sevengill on the head. It swirled away. Behind it was another shark approaching, and another.

Lindy tapped me on the shoulder. A shark I thought I recognized by its jerkiness of movement hurried toward us. Was it Crazy Junior, who had bitten the aeration trough yesterday? It looked like him, but I couldn't be sure. The sharks all looked pretty much the same right now, ugly, menacing, no friends of mine. I put one end of my scrub brush against the head of what might be Crazy Junior and guided the five-foot shark around us. He hurried off. I could not see where he went in the algae-clouded distance.

Attaching her suction cup to the window, Lindy started to scrub. The idea was that I would guard for Lindy while she scrubbed the first half of the thirty-two windows, and then we would trade jobs.

Everywhere I looked was a shark. It seemed impossible that

there were only thirteen of them. Like a parade of zombie sharks, the slow-moving sevengills came—straight toward the two divers on the wall.

Why? There was no blood in the water. We were not thrashing around or doing anything else I could think of that might excite a predator. Yet they would not leave us alone. I had to constantly turn and push and thump to keep the sharks away.

As we worked our way along the ascending line of hallway windows, the sharks swam beneath our kicking feet. Once a small sevengill got too close to Lindy's ankle, and I forgot my brush and grabbed the shark by the back of the head and pitched it. Sometimes there were several sharks coming at us at once, and I had to choose which shark to do something about. Often I had to tap Lindy on the shoulder so she could get involved.

The sharks showed no fear of us at all.

It was like the monster in your worst nightmare. It does not need to hurry, because you cannot get away.

Then I saw *her*, the biggest one, cruising along the line of windows. It was not difficult to recognize her, from her size and attitude, moving with an almost arrogant calm. Each side-to-side sway of her head sent a ripple of energy back through her body, releasing at the tail; each movement setting up the next, as if she were eternal. She looked as though she could never get tired, but would only swim and hunt forever.

She seemed everything I thought a shark should be: full of power, grace, capability. This was a sevengill with a capital S, I thought, and realized that would be a good name for her. I like to give private nicknames to special animals, but there was no need for that with her. She was just Sevengill, the summation of a species, and that was enough.

Sevengill. I said the name a couple of times to myself, testing the ring of it. Sevengill. She appeared not to notice how the other sharks hurried to get out of her way. I would happily have done the same, except we had to clean the windows.

The shark drew nearer. I admired the sculptured sweep of muscle along the middle of her back. Closer. I saw the gold-black eyes, the dark caverns of nostril on the edges of the broad brown snout, saw the white underside of the heavy lower jaw. I wished she would turn aside, but she showed no signs of doing so. She was now less than two body-lengths away from us.

What was I supposed to do? "Swim straight toward an approaching shark," one author recommended. I did not want to do that, feeling that she might take it as a challenge, but neither did I wish to appear defenseless.

When the shark's rough head was less than an arm's length away, I pushed the white bristle-brush hesitantly out. A little warning was all I intended. I expected her to flinch as the unfamiliar object came toward her face. Instead, the gold-black eyes disappeared.

Jaws yanked wide, teeth stood as though on hinges, and the suddenly eyeless head jerked six inches over, the gaping mouth pointed directly at me. She held that position for a freezing half-second, like a weapon drawn and aimed.

Then the eyes flickered, and came back. The mouth closed slowly. Neither accelerating her pace nor deviating from her path, Sevengill continued. If I had leaned forward, I could have touched the shark with my chest as she went by.

In a hundred years, or an hour, we finished and climbed out of the tank.

It had been a little better, but only a little, when Lindy was the guard. Then I did not have that awful sense of responsibility for someone else's life, feeling instead the warmth of having someone to look out for me. Even so, I could not relax. Every time I felt the vibrations of Lindy's wet-suited body lunging toward a shark beside me, I had to jerk around, nervous, ready to fight.

I am always scared before action, but seldom in the middle of it. This was different.

I was *afraid*, and I hated the sharks for making me feel that way.

When I am truly nervous, as I was then, nothing is so soothing as a walk around the world: Marine World/Africa USA. As soon as I got out of the tank that day, I dropped off my equipment and, still in my wet suit, headed off through the park. Since it was a winter weekday, the place was closed to the public. I felt as if the world belonged exclusively to me.

Marine World/Africa USA is like two circuses dumped into one. Its fifty-five acres in Redwood City made a complicated map, and there is no easy way to describe its layout. In the back, the service area, were the elephant barns, and also the training tanks where new dolphins and sea lion pups learned to offer natural behaviors in exchange for a fish. At a distance was a collection of pens for tigers, small cats, wolves when we had them (some animals were only visitors, here in between show business assignments). There was also a very tall shed for the giraffes when it rained. About a quarter of a mile beyond that came a construction building, the "cut shack" or food preparation room, and the dive locker, where I hung out when I was not in the water. Woven among all this was a many-armed lagoon.

And that was just the back of the park.

Beyond the dive locker was a bridge to the main part of Marine World, over which I headed now, walking so fast that water *squooshed* out of the tops of my rubber dive-suit booties, leaving feathery spray marks beside the flat wet footprints.

Smack! came a sound from underneath the bridge. It was Winston, the spotted harbor seal, slapping one flipper on the water's surface, ordering me to fetch him some fish. But I ignored his wishes, knowing he had been fed once already and would be brought food twice more before sunset; not to mention the school of smelt sharing the lagoon with him, which he could feed on if he were not too lazy to chase them. I wished the harbor seal could talk, to pass on some pointers on coexisting with sharks. But then, harbor seals are frequently found in the stomachs of sevengills, so maybe his advice would not be worth taking anyway!

On the other side of the bridge was Waldo, the talking water buffalo.

"Hi," said Waldo in a deep bass voice, guttural but clearly understandable through some accident of vocal cords and breathing muscles. His vocabulary was limited, but I had to admit he knew one more word of English than I knew of water buffalo. He probably did not know too much about sharks, though.

"Hi," said Waldo again as I waved and went by.

Heading past the arena where the African lion and Bengal tiger show was held in season, I stopped for a moment at Sea Lion Cove. Until they grow too old and slow, sea lions know how to cope with sharks. They just outswim them. Nothing can outmaneuver a sea lion in its prime; it has total flexibility to dodge and dart, and plenty of speed to zip away. I could not outswim anything except maybe another slow-swimming human like myself. Besides, in the end, the sharks get the sea lions, too.

As I went by the tall white pillars around the open-topped blue pools, I could almost hear the orca show's announcer starting up his spiel, and I remembered one part of his talk:

"Killer whales do not *have* enemies," he would say. "They *eat* them!" The great white shark might rarely reach a maximum of three thousand pounds and twenty feet. But even one of these would not dare bother a full-grown healthy orca, whales that routinely grow thirty feet in length and attain a weight of five tons. If I weighed ten thousand pounds and could swim as fast as an orca, I would not fear sharks either, I thought, at least until I got too old. In the end, of course, as with all ocean life, the killer whale's passing would be attended by sharks. They were the bringers of the end.

My footsteps slowed; I turned and headed back, toward my favorite nonhuman friend in the park.

His name was Gordo, and he rushed to the side of his tank when he saw me. A Pacific bottlenose dolphin, California cousin to the famous Atlantic bottlenose, only bigger, Gordo was ten feet long, and he raised a bow wave like a submarine. His name means "fat one" in Spanish, and it fit. The enormous animal weighed somewhere between six hundred and a thousand pounds. We did not have scales big enough to weigh him.

"Hi, you old fat thing," I said as the huge gray animal flipped over on his back, offering his belly to be scratched. I knew how he liked it, and scratched vigorously underneath his dolphin "armpits," so that he wriggled and opened his mouth and shut his eyes in ecstasy.

"You want a job as an anti-shark bodyguard?" I inquired.

One Navy scientist actually had tried to train a dolphin to kill sharks, as a bodyguard for frogmen. The dolphin cooperated as long as the sharks brought to him were of a species called browns, which are not very aggressive. But the day the scientist opened the sea gate to the dolphin's pen and let in a specimen of *Carcharhinus leucas*, commonly known as the bull shark, the project was over. There are sharks and *sharks*, and the dolphin knew the difference between the relatively placid browns he had been ramming to death and the aggressive and dangerous bull shark he would not get near.

Mostly, sharks and dolphins leave each other alone. Although both are fierce fighters, they do not usually seek violence when it can be avoided. I once saw film footage of a lemon shark wandering onto the scene of a dolphin birth. Instantly two male dolphins shot over to the shark. I thought, oh boy, there's going to be a fight. But no, the dolphins just got on both sides of the shark and shouldered it away, like two bouncers at a party gently ejecting a potential troublemaker.

From where I stood now I could see the shadowed opening to the reef aquarium hallway. I ignored it for a while, tugging Gordo back and forth by his tail, putting my hands around his huge beak, letting him wrestle me along the wall as I leaned over.

My wife had always been after me to become a teacher and give up diving professionally. I could do that. I nearly had my degree, and if I took up that line of work, I need never worry about sharks again. Like a person who stays off the road because he fears a car crash, I could be absolutely safe from sharks if I would only stay on land.

But I knew that was nonsense even as I thought it. The ocean was mine, and I would have it. Nothing would keep me away from that magnificent blue three-quarters of the world. I might be scared right now, but I would not live afraid. There had to be a way to live safely with the sharks, to get along: to understand.

Then I remembered something—a scared little face I had seen once when I had been scrubbing the reeftank windows. I guess to a four-year-old in his mother's arms I must have looked frightening: a blue-suited creature with a single glass "eye," bubbles roaring out of its face. The little boy took one look at me and hid his face in his mother's neck. You can imagine how I felt, to have maybe planted a fear of the ocean in an impressionable kid's mind. But then I had an idea. Waving frantically to keep the mother from going away, I pulled off my mask, pushed back my hood, and dropped my mouthpiece out. Smiling as hard as I could, I tried to show the kid that he had not seen a monster, but just a relatively normal human being. When I put my equipment back on and could see without a blur again, the little boy was looking at me. He was still ready to seek shelter with Mom if the need should arise, but he was looking at me now. Understanding had begun to take the place of fear.

I said good-bye to Gordo and headed for the windowed hallway that wound down around the reef.

It was dark inside. I was alone. The only sound was the soft *pad-padding* of my feet. Light from the tank windows rippled on the carpeting, and even in the dryness it was like being underwater.

I liked to take my children, Roman Jason Patrick and Desirée Don, to this spot and point out the different creatures, and try to hook their interest in the sea that links all nations. I showed them the giant seaweed called kelp, which can be ground up and converted into methane gas for energy, told them about fish farming as a way to increase the ocean's food yield, mentioned casually the fact that hamburgers and fried chicken were actually about half fish, because both cattle and fryers were raised on a diet forty to sixty percent fish meal—oh, my kids knew my ocean talks by heart!

The wall tanks filled one side of the hallway. There were the nonaggressive nurse sharks in their separate small tank. Beside them, the fish in the cold-water tank. Then the tropical fish tank with its technicolor inhabitants, and then the forty moray eels. Beside them were the giant sea bass, almost as big as the ones we once had in the reeftank across the hall, in the time when there were no sharks.

Every time I walked down this hallway I remembered why I was glad I worked not only for Marine World, but for the ocean as well. I certainly was not here for the money; there is no room for luxury on a park diver's pay. But nowhere else was there such an opportunity to work with ocean animals. Here I got stories to write, just from watching and paying attention. Here I liked to walk and dream, early in the morning. I loved this place. It summed up for me all the promise of the sea.

I did not notice the moving shadow on the carpeting at first, as it followed me along the row of reeftank windows.

It was just coincidence, of course, that Sevengill was passing by, filling up most of three windows as she came. I saw her dark length and the muscles, and the scars across her face. I looked into the eye that was closest to me and tried to guess her mind.

The eye was large and flat and oval, wedding-band gold around a spot of midnight. I could read nothing in it. What secrets she had, she kept.

If she noticed me at all, she gave no sign. Perhaps she was asleep, swimming automatically so that she would keep breathing. Or maybe, denied the scents and vibrations my living body would transmit in the water, I was just not real to her—a meaningless image on the glass, no more important than the wavering of light, or the passing of a cloud.

Feeding in Shark Alley

5

Three weeks later Keith Worcester and I were scrubbing the reeftank floor. Or rather, I was scrubbing, and Keith (brother of Dave Worcester, the killer-whale trainer) was taking his turn standing guard and being bored. For the moment the sharks were nowhere near, but we did not dare relax our vigilance.

In Keith's hand was a section of sawed-off broomstick with two nails pounded in one end: a light but effective shark stick, copied from a design of the famous undersea explorer, Jacques Cousteau. The blunt-headed nails would catch rough hide without cutting in, so a diver could poke off a shark without hurting it or making it mad.

The sevengills still acted exactly the same. Whenever divers went in to clean the reef windows, the slow-motion nightmare would commence—the sharks would swim right at us. No one had been hurt, but the situation felt unsafe, like an accident waiting to happen, as if we had been running across a crowded highway and so far our feet had not tripped.

Why did the sharks keep coming? Were they hungry, testing us out to see if we were something they should eat? Was it territoriality, where they simply wanted to get us out of their area? Or something else altogether?

I had read that most shark attacks are not triggered by hunger. Indeed, some scientists think sharks may not feel hunger pangs at all. Tests have shown that sharks who are starving are no more likely to bite a baited hook than are sharks with full bellies. So the fact that our sharks had not eaten in three weeks did not mean they were getting ready to attack us.

Also, sharks could go a very long time between meals, I reminded myself, looking back over my shoulder as I scrubbed. One big tiger shark in the Monaco aquarium went six months without eating—and then ate fifty pounds of a fish called blue runner in three days. For that matter, no shark ate very much. Their bodies are so perfectly streamlined that they do not need much energy to swim. Another big tiger shark, a species famed for its supposedly endless appetite, ate only one hundred ninety pounds of food in a year, which averaged out to just slightly more than half a pound of food a day. Of course, sharks did not average out their food but ate what they could, when they could—sometimes eating nothing, sometimes eating a lot. It crossed my mind that I weighed one hundred and ninety pounds.

Keith tapped my shoulder. I jumped.

The powerfully built blond diver held up his free hand and pointed to himself, then toward the wall, where I could dimly see some cruising sevengills, then back to where I was now standing. Wait here, I will be right back, I thought he meant. Apparently he had to get out for a moment, to go to the bathroom or something.

He returned in less than two minutes. He couldn't have climbed out of the tank and gotten his gear off in that short time. What was going on?

He beckoned me to follow.

All right. I swam between one of the hill-sized artificial reefs and the sunken boat toward the lower windows directly below the flume exit from the tank. Between us and the wall were sharks.

Holding up his hand for me to stop, Keith kept right on going. Swimming in between two heavy-bodied sevengills, he reached the wall safely, turned around, and *sat down*. He folded his arms. I had no idea what he was up to.

Sevengill cruised up to him. I tensed myself to spring to his assistance—and then the biggest shark went right on by.

Keith raised his arms like "See?" and patted the concrete companionably beside him. As if in a trance, I swam over and sat down also, and watched the sharks I feared swim slowly toward us—and past. It was astonishing. They might come within an inch of our faces, so that we could have scratched our chins on their rough backs, but they would always turn at the last moment, as if we were inanimate obstacles, just something in the way. They were not coming at us; we were where they wanted to be.

"They like the walls," said Keith afterward, and so it proved. Perhaps the walls reminded the sharks of a clifflike drop-off in the sea where the current struck and rose, swirling nutrients up from the ocean floor, attracting tiny planktonic creatures who liked to eat the nutrients, and bigger life forms who liked to eat the plankton. Or maybe the continuously swimming sharks simply found it easier to make the turn at the end of the tank if they took it wide, coming in right next to the walls.

Which is not to say the sharks' movements became completely predictable. Every cubic yard of water from surface to floor was their domain.

But if a shark was just ambling along, going no place in particular, the walls were where it would be, especially near the bottom. The area beside the lower windows became known to the divers as Shark Alley.

As the weeks went by and nothing happened, by which I mean no one was eaten, we began to think we had the sharks all figured out—that they were absolutely no threat to us anymore, that because the sharks had not bitten us, they never could, that we were somehow immune from the laws of the wild.

We quit guarding each other; moreover, we began to take chances with the sharks. Standing wide-legged in Shark Alley, we would let a smaller shark swim between our ankles. We posed for macho photographs, our fingers touching the sharks' rough sides as they swam by.

It was still strange to lift one's head and feel a scratchy stomach slide across as a shark went over, but that was just a momentary shiver.

I began to feel that sharks were harmless, and took delight in sharing this opinion with anyone I should happen to meet. If they did not bring up the subject, I would. I would echo the great Cousteau, saying "Sharks can be handled," making sure my listener understood that you had to know what you were doing, which of course we did, having swum with sharks for a whole two months now.

Even seeing my first shark kill did not teach me caution.

I had been working alone in the reeftank, vacuuming up piles of scrubbed-off algae left over from yesterday's work. This is an easy job, and one I enjoy. The siphon hose pulls the brown and purple chunks away as if by magic, and the mind is free to wander.

The light was wavering in its interconnected patterns, and at first everything was peaceful.

But gradually a sense of apprehension built around me, like the feeling you get when you walk into a room where people are just about to argue, and you can feel the tension building. Something was about to happen.

I looked over to the smaller of the two artificial reefs. In the pocket of the L-shaped reef, a green-and-white-striped kelp bass eighteen inches long lay twitching spasmodically, arching head and tail together, as if trying to rid itself of some internal pain.

I knew this particular fish. It had come from Santa Monica, California, where the water is badly polluted. The kelp bass had cancer. Just as with humans, pollution causes cancer in fish, and an ugly white growth had built up into a blockage of the fish's throat. It could no longer swallow. I had tried to feed it the day before yesterday, and the piece of food would drop right out, however many times the kelp bass gulped it in.

I wanted to kill the poor little thing, to end its suffering quickly. I was not supposed to; the park's policy was to let sick fish alone and give them every possible chance to recover. But this fish wasn't going to get better. No way. Regulations or not, I would just have to go get a canvas bag, swoop up the bass, bonk it on the head with something, and put it out of its pain.

But if I was slowed by regulations, there was another in the tank who was not.

Crazy Junior circled in, his every movement poised and ready.

This was what the shark was made for. In, around, away, the figure-eighting pattern tightened, the sevengill watching not only its prospective victim, but also for what might come up from behind. Whenever anything in the ocean hunts, it had best be on its guard. One small lapse in caution, and the hunter can become the hunted.

As in a dance, a prearranged pattern of movement and possible responses, the prelude to killing continued. When the shark's rough fin brushed by, did the kelp bass dash away, as a healthy fish would have done? It did not. When the wide mouth opened, did the weapon-spines which boned the bass's fins stand up and stab? They did not.

The shark scooped up the cancerous fish. Limply, it lay across the jaws. Teeth like crystal thorns tapped lightly on the bass's back and sides, but there was no response.

Abandoning delicacy, Crazy Junior shook his head and bit the bass in two. Almost. A thread of tough belly skin connected the body of the kelp bass inside the shark's mouth to the tail, which was still out. Back and forth that tail fin flopped, jerking to the rhythm of the shark's shaking head.

I became aware that I was getting too absorbed in the scene before me. A tingle rose in the back of my neck.

I spun, and the biggest shark in the tank was where she had no business being. I was not by the walls. There was no reason for her to be here, with her mouth just beginning to yawn. From so close the gap between her jaws looked big enough to take my shoulders in.

I flopped backward quickly and brought my knees up to fight, but Sevengill had already turned away. Her motion seemed abrupt, angry, as if she had been cheated.

*　　*　　*

Snick, snick, snick. My knife converted three herring to a pile of neat pink ovals on the wooden tray. I brushed the cut fish aside and reached for more.

I was standing in the cleanest room of Marine World. Twice a day the gleaming stainless steel sinks and concrete floors were soaped, mopped with an antiseptic cleanser, and hot-water rinsed to sterility. It had to be so, for this was the cut shack, where the animals' food was prepared. Any uncleanliness here might mean sickness to an animal.

The pile of cut fish grew swiftly. I finished slicing with a sigh and a shake of the head.

Winter was gone, spring was half over, and still the sharks had not eaten—not the way I wanted them to.

The best way for a predator to feed is to catch and eat the sick and the stupid, the crippled and the dying fish, as Crazy Junior had done. In this way sharks benefit the sea, limiting the spread of disease and keeping the ocean healthy. The strong survive to reproduce, and those too weak to catch their own food are prevented from suffering. This setup was fine for our sharks as long as there were a few sick fish available.

But when these easiest targets were used up, what then? In the wild, sevengills like ours would go after other sharks, and stingrays. We had found evidence this was happening in our tank, too.

A fragment of leopard shark tail found drifting across the bottom one morning told us that at least some of the sevengills were making dietary arrangements. Also the stingrays had all disappeared, in installments. First, the wide-winged swimmers would be missing their stingers, a sharp, notch-edged spine at the base of the long whippy tail. A couple of days after that, the rest of the stingray would vanish.

But we did not know *which* sharks were eating. Was everybody getting enough food?

I really wanted the sevengills to eat the food we offered them so we could keep a watch on who ate how much, and when. There was also another reason, which I was just a little embarrassed to admit, why I wanted the sharks to eat the frozen and thawed mackerel, herring, smelt, or squid we gave them: I liked the little animals of our reef and did not want them to be eaten. It was not logical, but that was how I felt.

I was no scientist, required to be objective about my feelings. Some of the stingrays that were getting eaten now I had tamed till they would nestle on my hands like big butterflies and take squid from my fingers. Stingrays, if you look close, have a smile as cute as the old cartoon character Casper the Friendly Ghost, and it made me sad when one got eaten. My thinking is that when we humans take an animal from the wild and keep it captive for our pleasure and education, we then become responsible for its well-being. Being eaten before one's normal lifespan was over did not seem like a fair deal to me.

Even Steinhart Aquarium, one of the greatest gathering places of oceanic knowledge in the world, had had trouble at first feeding the shark I knew as Sevengill. As we had done at Marine World, the scientists had tossed in a variety of flavorsome edibles right on top of the shark, the fish chunks drifting down around her, tantalizing her with the coppery scent of blood—and she ignored them. Even divers going in and placing food directly on the floor before her had done no good.

And then one Steinhart scientist tried to start a growth experiment with a three-foot leopard shark. The man had caught the black-and-gray shark in the bay, tagged it with a yellow piece of plastic marker in the dorsal fin, and tossed it into the doughnut-shaped Roundabout tank where Sevengill was. The project was not supposed to include Sevengill, but she got involved anyway.

"She hit that leopard shark like a Polaris missile, tore it in two, and ate both pieces," aquarium director Dr. John McCosker said of the incident. "After that we had no trouble feeding her or the others. We just kept a supply of leopard sharks in the tank and let the sevengills feed themselves in the natural way, as they do in the wild."

It was logical when he explained it that way. But still I did not want our sevengills to eat the other creatures in the tank.

Also, I would feel a bit more comfortable if I was positive the sharks had full stomachs all the time.

I wanted the sharks to take their food from us—only how? When we threw the food in from the side, the slow-to-get-excited sevengills were apt to be left out. As soon as the bucketfuls of chopped mackerel, herring, river smelt, and squid flopped down on the surface of the tank, sea gulls swooped down, and striped bass shot up, and leopard sharks snatched any food that reached the floor. By the time the sevengills got interested, everything was gone.

Some aquariums put fish on the end of long poles and reached down from the sides of the aquarium walls to feed their surface-feeding sharks. But the sevengills swam low in the tank, usually, and our walls were high. The feeding sticks would have to be about thirty feet long, which would be a little difficult to maneuver.

What was I supposed to do, I wondered as I pulled more fish from the cut-shack freezer—shove the food down the throats of the sharks? Steinhart diver Norval Greene had done that, and I remembered the picture of the scar he got for his troubles. I was not going to try force-feeding.

The forty-pound gray plastic feed tray filled up at last with a raw seafood smorgasbord—chopped river smelt and silver herring, whole pink squid with staring eyes and long white tentacles, and foot-long Pacific mackerel stacked at one side. How could any self-respecting shark pass up a chance at that?

I heard familiar footsteps coming up behind me. Only one person I knew bounced through life quite like that, and I grinned as I turned to John Racanelli. The happy-faced diver with the physique of a compressed gorilla was holding one of our shark sticks.

"I figured out how to feed the sharks," he said. "You put a fish on the end of the stick, and poke the fish inside the shark's mouth. I tried it on Sunday, and it works great."

"Why didn't you wait and let me back you up?" I said, trying to be mad. "You know we're supposed to have someone else along when we try anything different and maybe dangerous."

"What if you had said no?" he replied with perfect logic, ducking as I threw a squid at him.

Which was why, ten minutes later, I hung in the coolness just over the bottom in that part of the reeftank called Shark Alley.

In one hand was the canvas feeding sack, almost empty. I had dropped off most of the chopped fish and squid, dumping pieces at strategic intervals throughout the tank, to give the turtles something to keep busy with for a while. A diver who went into the reef with food had to plan on being aggressively visited by the table-sized green sea turtles. They could move with surprising velocity; "slow as a turtle" is false in the sea. And their appetites?

In winter they ate almost nothing. In spring and summer they almost never stopped, and you had best count your fingers if they got too close.

A shark more gray than brown zipped near. I reached into the canvas sack, pulled out a twelve-inch Pacific mackerel, popped it on the shark stick's nails, and poked it at Crazy Junior's face.

Whack! The gray-brown head jumped over and I heard the grate of teeth on the nails. The stick became light. I watched Crazy Junior deal with the mackerel he had taken, saw the eyes flicker as the mouth flipped the fish around till it pointed headfirst down the throat. Junior shook once, the tail dropped softly to the floor, and the rest went where good food goes.

Racanelli's idea worked great!

Every shark that came near got a fish poked at its face. When the bulge of cheeklike muscle at the joining of the jaws was touched, the result was instantaneous: a six-inch blur of movement, ending at the fish.

This must be how some shark attacks happen, I thought. The shark and human are moving through dark or murky water where neither can see clearly, and they just bump into each other. Maybe a bare foot slides into the tooth-rimmed mouth, and the shark bites by reflex. A pretty good argument for not swimming at night or in filthy water.

There she was, Sevengill, and I didn't have a fish on the stick yet. But I thought I knew how far her head would yank over, and I wanted to feed her by hand. She might hurt her teeth on the nails, I told myself, as I held out the fish by the tail. Her jaws came together, *whonk*, like manhole covers meeting.

An always hungry (and nearsighted) turtle slammed into the back of my neck. It must have smelled the food. I knew imme-

diately who it was and plunged my free hand back to get hold of the stupid reptile. It bit my fingers. I shook free, grabbed the wrinkled neck, pulled the water-light armored thing over my head and away—and *another* green sea turtle came, with a moray eel swimming underneath, using the turtle as moving cover. The second turtle got so excited at the nearness of food that it slammed right into Sevengill, knocking her over. Her white belly showed—and then she was gone.

The moray wriggled swiftly out from under the turtle and arrowed toward me. Bulbous nostrils in the narrow head detected food. I reached deep into my canvas bag, found a mackerel, and held it out. Teeth like slivers of glass snatched the fish. Five feet of yellow-brown eel rotated and sliced the mackerel's head off, letting it fall and engulfing the rest. As I passed out more fish to the eternally hungry turtles, I noticed that Sevengill had not been so upset as to drop her fish when she left the area.

I was very glad the confusion had not happened with Crazy Junior. He did not appear to have the bigger Sevengill's confidence and might have panicked, snapping at anything in reach. The two sharks had very different temperaments.

We had begun to be able to tell the sharks apart, not only by the way they looked, but also by how they acted.

Sharks, it seems, have personality.

Life Among the Sharks

6

~~~~~~

Can sharks have individual personalities?

Some people would say no, arguing that these primitive fish have brains too small for individuality. But to me, brain size is only one ingredient in personality. In the microscopic world of a drop of water, for instance, no life form is big enough to have a brain at all. Yet even here, behavior can vary. Some amoebas seek the light more than others do.

Other people will say that seeing personality in sharks is an-thropomorphic: believing animals to be "just like people," which can lead to misunderstanding.

Like the mistake I made with the electric, or torpedo, ray, Latin-named *Torpedo nobiliana*. For years I thought that the four-foot gray pancake of a fish was evil-tempered, deserving the nickname of Uncle Ugly because he would thump into us divers again and again, giving us an electric shock every time. The pain was excruciating, especially when we were zapped on the head, where it felt like red-hot nails being pounded into the brain. But, as we finally realized, the electric ray wasn't being ferocious; he was just nearly blind. Uncle Ugly's beady black eyes were apparently for decoration only. When he blundered into us and turned on the voltage, he was probably reacting more from fear than irritability.

Trying to detect personality in sharks without misinterpreting their behavior was hard enough. But there was also the problem of time. As a working diver I could not watch the sharks every moment I was in the tank with them; there was too much head-down floor-scrubbing work to be done. It would have been great if a scientist could have studied our sharks systematically over the years. He or she could have set up a chair in the aquarium hallway, watching through a window to monitor and record, writing down exactly what each shark did. Then we would have known much better what made each animal unique.

Yet even with these difficulties, we began to be able to tell the sharks apart and to spot the differences which in my opinion made character.

The Shy One, Socrates, and Crazy Junior were three medium-length sevengill sharks, five to six feet long, all looking more or less alike. Each had the typical sevengill color pattern, like badly baked bread, brown on top and doughy white below. There were a few visual dissimilarities—Socrates had a banged-up snout, Crazy Junior was more gray than brown, and the Shy One was thicker through the body than the others. But it was the differences in the way they acted that most interested me.

The Shy One lived up to his nickname from the first moment I touched him, pushing him out from the entryway flume the day he arrived. He had lain so quietly in the arrival stretcher that

I thought maybe he was sick, possibly dying. Even in the water he stayed as limp as a pile of wet laundry. After I shoved him out into the reef, I snatched up a mask and followed him with my eyes, expecting to have to go help him start swimming. The Shy One hung still in the water for a long moment, his body all hunched together, as if he were afraid to offend anyone—and then he dashed off as if swimming for his life.

From then on what we mainly saw of the Shy One was his tail, because he was always going away. If we even looked at him too hard he would run, which made him a difficult animal to feed by hand. We had to pretend that shark feeding was the furthest thing from our minds—not even glancing in his direction—and, when he got near enough, bump the food accidentally into his mouth, which would trigger the bite reflex. The Shy One was also the first shark to learn to take food off the floor, which he preferred to receiving it from us.

Socrates was named after an ancient Greek wise man. This was a joke because our Socrates was *dumb*. Not that we expected intelligent conversation, but was it too much to expect a shark that got breath by motion to keep swimming? Socrates liked to poke his head into small holes from which he could not get out. Perhaps he had once caught a fish or an eel in a cave and had been trying to repeat this trick ever since. I do not know. But time and again we would find Socrates with his head jammed firmly into a crack or crevice or small cave in one of the artificial reefs. His tail would be lashing determinedly as if he thought he was going somewhere. As sharks cannot swim backward, he would be stuck until a nervous diver pulled him loose. Stupid or not, Socrates was still a five-foot shark with perfectly operational teeth. But he never seemed to resent our attentions. He would just swim calmly away and hunt himself another hole. The skin got

rubbed off his nose, exposing white flesh and cartilage beneath. Like the scars of a boxer, it sounds worse than it looked, but the wound never healed.

And as for Crazy Junior, the shark who had turned around and come back snapping the first morning we met—he was strange. I have since read that certain small sharks are especially aggressive in their younger years and mellow out as they grow old, if they live that long. In the wild, larger sharks will take advantage of these smaller, more aggressive individuals. They watch and wait to see what will happen when a little one makes a move at a questionable target, such as a sick whale that might be dying or might not. If the younger, quicker shark gets eaten or otherwise discouraged, the big ones will go off about their business without having had to risk themselves, profiting from the mistake of a shark like Crazy Junior.

Sometimes the actions of Crazy Junior seemed insane, dangerous, and possibly destructive to himself. But were there shark-sense reasons for what he did? Maybe when he bit the aeration trough the first day I saw him, he was just responding to the metal in the trough itself, which his electrically sensitive ampullae of Lorenzini detected. (We know now that one reason great white sharks bite moviemakers' antishark cages is the metal bars themselves. Metal gives out a mild electric charge which the shark may interpret as something alive. Add to that the hundreds of gallons of blood the filmmakers have poured on top of the antishark cages, and it becomes more understandable why "whitey" will mouth the cage bars, searching for the wounded animal that is leaking all that juice.)

Maybe Crazy Junior's aggressiveness would have been entirely logical—to another shark. But what the pugnacious animal reminded me of was one of those people who hang out in bars, waiting for someone to pick a fight with. Such needlessly rowdy folks do not make sense to me, but they exist, and so did Crazy Junior.

He would bite *anything*. Maybe he got information from his teeth. I don't know. But he would mouth a diver's wet-suited arm when we fed him fish, so that we would have to thump his head.

Once I watched that shark try to catch a kelp bass resting on a window sill, miss the catch, and bite the window sill repeatedly after the kelp bass was gone.

Another time he tried to eat Chopper, our five-hundred-pound loggerhead sea turtle. This was a challenge, as Chopper's shell is roughly one and a half inches thick. Even so, she did not take it lightly when the shark ran his teeth along her armored side. Apparently there are nerve endings in turtle shell, because she spun like a dial, flinging him off. Crazy Junior persisted, coming back again and again. But when he grabbed the sea turtle's right front flipper in his mouth and commenced to shake violently back and forth, trying to bite off the nonretractable "arm," Chopper bit back. The triangular beak yawned wide and snapped, removing a piece from Crazy Junior's high-lobed tail. The shark let go of the turtle without delay.

Once I was struggling to remove my wet-suit jacket underwater. My awkward motions must have reminded Crazy Junior of a wounded fish, because he circled in tight around me as he had done to the cancerous kelp bass. I had to thump him hard to convince him I was in good health, with no need of his attentions.

But the shark whose personality I really wanted to get in touch with was the largest one, Sevengill. Partly it was her size that drew me. I have always liked big things: lions, mountains, weight lifters, whales. I found myself frequently looking for Sevengill, wondering what she was up to. As she passed seven feet in length and began to grow even more in strength and massiveness, I admired her power and wished she knew me.

She had a great natural calmness and poise, a dignity like that of the ocean itself.

Once I stood up too quickly from my scrubbing and Sevengill, who had been just about to swim over me, bumped right into my chest. She neither panicked nor became aggressive. She simply held still for a second to see what the situation required, and then she went around me. Sharks do not have the facial muscles to give a range of expressions, but I felt that she understood I intended no harm. Her body language remained calm, and also I felt there was another kind of signal.

Scientists say animals and people send out brain waves all the time. I believe these waves can be received through some form of extrasensory perception, and so I always try to "listen" to what an animal is thinking. It is guessing, of course, but most people who work with animals will tell you that they try to do it just the same.

Another measure of the sharks' personalities was how they interacted with the reef's other animals.

Like the eight-inch mother garibaldi, fierce as a spark of orange fire. She had a nest made of carefully groomed living red algae, protecting her hundreds of tiny gold-dot eggs. Once, before I learned where the nest was, I swam right up beside it and felt a pain in my jacketless armpit as if someone had stuck me with an automobile's red-hot cigarette lighter. I looked up and saw Mother Garibaldi spit out a sixteenth-inch cube of me. After that I remembered where her nest was.

The garibaldi's nest lay on the floor very close to the customary path of the sharks. I took to spending time near the nest when I could, watching what happened when the sharks swam by. I knew from books that garibaldis will nip sharks who come near their nests in the wild—but what would the sharks do?

I saw the orange mother fish dart out and nip the Shy One on the gills. It panicked him. He fled in a rush.

Socrates reacted professorially, flinching at each repeated nip, but investigating nonetheless, studying the yellow-dot eggs in the nest before rejecting them as too small a snack for the trouble.

When Momma Garibaldi pecked at Crazy Junior, he spun and charged the reef, slamming into the fiberglass where the little fish had been. I always wondered what would happen when they met again, but I never saw.

And Sevengill? She saw the nest before she got there and swam casually around it. Mother Garibaldi also pulled back a little bit, as if in recognition of authority.

Sevengill. When I was a kid I was underweight and picked on, and I used to fantasize I owned a giant dog called a brindle mastiff. I would name him Jad, after Tarzan's golden lion in Edgar Rice Burroughs's books. I figured if any bullies came around, I would tell Jad to eat them. In a way, Sevengill aroused that same remembered wish: a yearning for an animal that nobody else could get near, that no one but I could control.

I began to feel that Sevengill was mine in a way, that I owned her, or that we were—well—friends.

I liked to touch her as she swam by, and she tolerated it. I never restricted her motion, no more than would a stroke of seaweed brushing against her side. I knew better than to make her feel trapped in any way. Once I had watched disbelieving as a longtime diver who should have known better actually pulled one of our sharks by the tail. The shark spun around and snapped its jaws together. If the tail-puller had not had luck and the swiftness of terror, he might have lost his hand.

I told myself Sevengill allowed more liberties from me than she would from anyone else. I would tease her sometimes with a fish, drawing her around in a circle till she tired of the frustrating game and lunged, and her teeth came together with an audible clunk.

Once I tried to make a home movie starring the sharks. The hero (for whom I was doing the stunt work) was to rescue a woman astronaut whose space capsule had crashed in the ocean. The villain, who just happened to be around, had supposedly excited the sharks with low-pitch vibrations like wounded fish make. I was supposed to chase the sharks off and wrestle one by way of variety.

I figured I would do the wrestling scene first to get it over with. Wearing swim trunks and a face mask, I swam down into Shark

Alley. A diver beside me held an air hose I could use between filmings, and I kept my mask in place until the shark I had chosen to wrestle came close. Of course I picked the Shy One. I took an enormous breath, removed my face mask, and lunged at the blur. Catching up to the slow-moving shark, I wrapped my arms around him. For an instant the Shy One held absolutely still and I thought I had gotten away with it. Then the shark started to move. I could not hang on. His skin points were smooth aiming back toward the tail, and maybe there is some light healthy oil on the skin of a shark, but for whatever reason, I could not maintain my grip. The shark slipped gradually from my fingers and turned, and his head whipped back and forth, slamming like a baseball bat against both sides of my head, *bam, bam, bam*. But fortunately he did not bite, and only broke away.

Next we filmed the astronaut's escape from our homemade chicken-wire space capsule, then we did the last of the stunt work down in Shark Alley. The sevengills swam by as always, having no idea they had just become movie villains. I would swim out and "chase them away," spreading my arms wide and bumping my chest up against them. Naturally this unexplainable behavior spooked them, and one after another they took off in a fright— until I tried it on Sevengill.

The big shark was lumbering by with her quicker-than-it-seemed slow cruising when I swam after her. It took me a little time to catch up, and when I came nearer the dark blurry out-line, I could see her shape changing as she kept looking back, seemingly puzzled. When I continued to approach, she stopped. And turned around. Even without my mask to give me a clear view, her body language was plain, and the feeling I got unmis-takable.

Clear as if written in print, the thought crossed between us: You are not even *thinking* about bothering me, are you?

No, ma'am, hunh-uh, not me. I stopped and held still, and she turned away.

"She sure looked at you weird," said Dave Di Fiore, the photographer, afterward.

But even this small embarrassment did not quell my growing confidence. When I saw a picture of a diver feeding a shark in the wild mouth-to-mouth, holding a fish between his teeth and giving it to a small reef shark that way, I had to duplicate the stunt.

Holding a mackerel between my teeth, I waited till Sevengill was near. She would eat only one or two fish every couple of days, but this looked like the day. I shoved my face toward hers. She hesitated, but then she took the fish. Hard. I had misjudged the distance and our mouths met in a numbing "kiss" which felt more like a door opening up against my face, bruising my lips against my own teeth.

I did not repeat that particular foolishness.

The months flew faster, and became years. Socrates died, having wedged himself so deeply in a hole that he strangled. Suicide by stupidity. We found him stiff and stark in the morning, sticking up out of the top of one of the reefs, bent over halfway like a flag at half-mast to himself.

Crazy Junior bit one animal too many. We spotted Uncle Ugly, the electric ray, first, rippling clumsily around the windows. The reason for his clumsy speed was some still-bleeding parallel gouges furrowed on his side. Then we found Crazy Junior. He was lying on the floor, belly up, looking as dead as when we first met. But there would be no bringing him back this time. It must have been like sticking your tongue into a wall socket when he bit the ray: electrocution.

Over the years we found out a little bit more about shark intelligence. Once I got to help catch two small sevengills that were to be returned to Steinhart Aquarium. The first shark we tricked with a wall of nets held by a team of divers. They herded the shark up to the shallow flume, where men with a stretcher waited and calmly scooped it up. No problem.

That trick worked only once; then the other sharks got wise. We tried for an hour and they would not come near the nets again. Maybe it was only a coincidence, but it seemed like pretty quick learning to me.

We still had to catch the other shark. Back down in Shark Alley, I was able to slip a hand-held pole net over the head of a four-foot sevengill. However, the shark struggled so hard that it broke the handle and hoop of the net. I wrapped my legs around the shark just before it shook off the wrecked restraint. Locking my arms around the upper half of the terrified creature, I started to swim awkwardly up to the flume.

The shark twisted around and bit me on the wet-suited fore-arm. Fortunately my legs were restricting its motion and it could not thrash back and forth, which greatly diminished its biting power. But as you might imagine, I was not altogether happy. The shark's head was still glommed onto my arm, and my body and legs were still wrapped around the shark, as the tangle of human and fish reached the flume.

"I could use some help down here," I said to a man standing in the flume. But he only looked at the shark on my arm, and his eyes got real big and he said, "Let it go." Let it go? And have to go through this all over again? Not likely! I waited until the stretcher was brought over and then gave the shark to the stretcher carriers. Holding on did not show courage on my part, but simple stubbornness. I am a good animal catcher and would have been embarrassed to let go of something after I had it safely caught. Afterward I examined my sleeve, which looked like multiple razors had been at play. But the teeth had not touched my arm. This near escape from serious injury added to my growing feelings of invulnerability.

The years went by and nobody was seriously injured. There was only an occasional scratch or two incurred in feeding when we misjudged the return of the sharks' biting heads and got lightly raked across the knuckles. We divers came to feel we knew the sharks as individuals. The confidence we felt around them reached unhealthy levels. It became difficult for us to take the sharks seriously. Like longtime commuters on the freeway who may no longer worry about the dangers of the road, we were taking the sharks for granted. It was as if we swam in invisible armor and the sharks could never hurt us. Even when we were reminded of their capabilities, we paid almost no attention.

We found their teeth on the floor every day, both the slender piercing needles of the upper teeth and the sawing cutters of the underjaw. This did not mean our sharks were going toothless; it was typical shark-tooth progression: loss and replacement. Like bullets in a clip, shark teeth are stacked one on top of each other in rows inside the jaw, and are slowly moving up and outward all the time. Each tooth moves to the outer edge of the jaw, where it is in position for biting, then migrates a little farther and drops out. Imagine getting a new set of teeth every couple of weeks!

Sevengill teeth are not impressive to look at, especially the

sawlike lower teeth, but they are actually some of the most efficient slicers in the shark kingdom, as one poor diver found out.

"How sharp can this be?" he said, holding the half-inch lower
jaw tooth to the light.

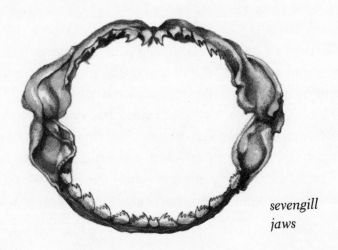

*sevengill
jaws*

If he had waited, I would have shown him how that insignificant little chip could slice paper as cleanly as a razor blade. But
our friend was the impatient kind and swiftly scratched the tooth
across his palm, which split open. There was considerable excitement before we found some clean towels and stopped the
flow of blood.

And one day we had another demonstration of what those
teeth could do.

We found the body of a five-foot sevengill shark on the bottom
of the reeftank. The shark was torn nearly in two. The internal
organs and genitals were gone, as well as almost a third of the
animal, from one tremendous bite. The tough cartilaginous spi-
nal column which serves the shark as backbone was sheared

completely through. As we took the shark out, I remembered how hard it had been to open and clean a leopard shark I had once caught as a small boy on a fishing trip. The tough skin and muscle had dulled a sharp knife, and it had required all my strength to force the point of the blade into the belly of the little leopard shark.

But this bite mark was clean and neat, as if the meat had been frozen and sawed. The half-moon shape of missing flesh was fifteen inches across and nine inches into the animal. There was no question in my mind which shark had done it.

A friend posed for the camera, kneeling behind the shark's gutted body. As the diver joked and smiled for the picture, I could not help noticing how easily his folded knee would have fit inside the wound, which corresponded to the radius of Sevengill's jaws.

The Man Who Gets Sharks in the Mail

7

~~~~~~

One gray and still November morning in 1979, an electrical storm began to build. There was a faint buzz and sputtering in the air, like the crackle one hears around high-tension wires. All across Marine World the delicate senses of the animals responded. Two giraffes fought a slow-motion neck war; a normally easy-going Shetland pony screamed and reared and kicked out at nothing; the challenge of an African lion—*mwaaaoh!*—echoed like thunder.

When I went into the grouper tank to add a little more sand, the giant sea bass boomed their warning signal—*CHUNK! CHUNNK!*—and the spines stood up on their gray-green backs. In the dolphin tank the normally friendly dolphins jaw-snapped at me and *zwooshed* their tail flukes just short of my face, stopping the crunching blow an inch from concussion like a deadly game with a baseball bat.

It started to rain as I climbed out of the dolphin tank. I felt the separate droplets hitting me, and my reaction was odd, as though normality were reversed: the air was wet, so I should go back underwater, where it was dry. I heard a rumble in the distance from a lightning bolt I had not seen.

Before going in to scrub the reeftank windows, I watched the sky for a moment or two. I was looking for a little more of what passes for lightning in northern California—spills of bright light in the towering clouds, interesting but not spectacular. Nobody worries about Bay Area lightning, but still I hesitated before clambering down the wet redwood steps into the reeftank flume.

With a *shlup!* like a frog's tongue encasing an insect, the water closed over my head.

Almost at once, even as I swam from the entryway across the long open stretch of the reeftank to the farthest, and uppermost, windows, where they began their descending spiral around the wall, I could feel the strange acrid tension continuing to build.

As I attached suction cup to window, I felt my breathing grow short. The air behind my mask smelled flat and dead. Probably the filter cartridges needed changing, I told myself, trying to ignore the impinging evidence of all my senses.

Then I remembered the time years before, when I had felt this same sense of anticipation, a tenseness in the water, like the hum of a wire drawn too tightly, vibratinnggg–snap! An actual noise had broken the tension back then, and I had turned and seen a moray eel in the middle of its kill. A kelp bass had wandered too close to the moray's cave, and the snap was the sound of the fish's back breaking.

Was something hunting in the reef today? I turned away from the glass, remembering the eel kill, wondering if some fish was about to be eaten.

Around me was a sea of fast-moving sharks. This was not right. Usually the sharks preferred to cruise near the lower end of the windows, in Shark Alley. But not now. Every sevengill in the tank seemed to be up here with me, none of them more than twenty feet away.

The leopard sharks on the floor traded places nervously, ready to dash away quick. The orange mother garibaldi flickered closer to the overhanging fiberglass reef, her hideout in case of trouble. A school of kelp bass collected in their hiding pattern, looking like waving seaweed. Even old warrior-fish One-Eye, the massive red-and-black sharp-toothed sheephead, backed partway into his hole in the side of the hollow reef.

The freezing water was very clear; I could see the darkness of the square-cut flume hole in the wall on the other side of the tank. It was only fifty feet of swimming to that exit, not very far. Even with all my gear on I could swim it in five or six seconds, as easily as a person can run fifteen yards on a football field if there are no tacklers in the way.

I was getting nervous for nothing, I told myself, and there were thirty-two windows to clean. Some of the upper windows had scratches in the plastic covering the multilayered glass, and I pinched several nylon brush bristles between thumb and forefinger to delicately clean the algae from the shallow gouges.

Thump! A shark slammed into the back of my calf, numbing and knotting the muscle. It was no accidental bump. I thought I was bitten. I spun around, pulling my legs up in front of me, rubbing where the shark had struck.

The sharks all looked like Crazy Junior had just before he killed the cancerous kelp bass: alert, alive, hunting. Gone was the zombielike cruising. These animals hurtled back and forth violently fast, changing directions in the flick of an instant.

It was happening—that thing which every diver most dreads. The sharks had begun to frenzy.

I had seen film footage of this destructive phenomenon, when sharks get a sudden abundance of food and appear to go crazy, snapping and tearing at anything. In the footage I saw, the sharks got so excited there was soon nothing to see but hurtling brown bodies and finally just a blur of froth and bubbles. It was said that in this state, sharks will bite each other, or even bite themselves.

A frenzy should not be happening now. The sharks had no reason to act so excited. There was no blood in the water, no explosions of sound, no violent or strange motions.

I wanted to get out. But how? If I left the wall, my back would be unprotected. The rain-broken surface just above me was an empty promise, the worst place to be in case of shark attack. The only time a fish heads for the air is when it is hunting or escaping, and fleeing means weakness. But closer to me, on the far side of one of the fiberglass reefs, there was a broken spot, a cave, just big enough for a diver to crawl inside. I could reach it in seconds. The morays who lived there would not object. They were civilized creatures; we could work things out.

A shark wriggled between my neck and the wall, nipped at my hood, and was gone. I whacked my elbow up but missed. It was too late to retreat to the cave. Now there was only time to do what a cornered animal must: fight.

Backing as far as possible into the four-inch recession of the window, I turned the scrub brush around in my hand so that the handle stuck out between my knuckles.

A five-foot shark rushed in, open-mouthed. I thumped it with the brush handle. It felt like punching a telephone pole. The

shark bent and flashed off in a swirl of motion. Others came in. We fought.

The safe and civilized part of me went away. I was alive in a way no sheltered man can ever be. My body surged with strength. I was too excited to be scared.

My method of defense was simple. Curled up with my back against the glass, I hit anything rough that came near. The smaller sharks were the more aggressive. Sometimes there was more than one to deal with at once, so that I was hitting and kicking at the same time, thumping and whacking for all I was worth.

Strange, but even at the height of excitement a part of me was distant, uninvolved, watching. It seemed the same was true for the sharks. They knew what they were doing every minute, as if some group communication linked them. Even in frenzy, they never lost control. No matter how quickly they moved—and they moved like brown bullets—they were not crazy mad, snapping at each other. They were aware and intelligent; sometimes they even seemed to be taking turns. Everything happened at a speed I could just barely cope with. No shark completely threw caution away; each one held back just a little, wanting not only to bite, but also to get away clean.

I felt I had been practicing for this. We had developed a shark feeding show we did once a day in summer, and this felt like that, only faster, with the sharks coming in two or three at a time and me handing out punches and kicks instead of Pacific mackerel. A swelling exultation grew inside me as I fought and fought and was not harmed. It began to seem possible for me to prevail, to win a nice clean draw with nobody hurt.

Then the lesser sharks got out of the way, and I saw *her*, Sevengill, nearly eight feet long, coming along the line of windows. Everything about her spelled *shark*—from her desk-sized head with the upside-down U slash of her jaws extending well down the sides of her neck, to the mass of muscle through her middle which would add to the pressure of her bite, to the stiff and sweeping power of her high-lobed tail. She came in closer, and I remembered how that dead shark had looked after she had bitten through its stomach and spine.

At the last she turned to go around me. She might even have left me alone altogether. I will never know. I was tired of feeling hunted, and I kicked her in the side of the head.

The fintip curled under; the ball of my foot caught her like a fist just in front of the gills. I felt the corner of her jaws beside my toes. Her head snapped back and for one icy instant I thought she would take my leg. Then incredibly her mouth slammed together above my shins, and the shark exploded into motion which my eyes couldn't follow. If she had struck me at that speed I would have had no chance to dodge or deflect her. If she had hit the surface she would have leaped into the air.

When I could see her clearly again, she was across the tank and turning, coming back. I felt like a boxer who has just thrown his knockout punch and his opponent smiles. All I had to offer was more of the same. As she came closer I wondered dumbly if I was reflected in the pupil of her black-and-yellow eye.

Sevengill's body relaxed; her motion slowed and calmed. She turned an underwater corner, looked me over with no particular excitement, and then seemed to dismiss the whole subject of divers.

As if at a signal, the tension eased in the tank. The group aggression was over. The whole event must have taken no more than three or four minutes.

The kelp bass unstrung themselves from their imaginary hiding place; Mother Garibaldi came out from under her overhang; One-Eye the sheephead emerged from his cave and charged a young intruder, which fled.

Above me the rain beat down harder. When I poked my head above the tank surface for a second, the feeling of lightning was gone. I finished scrubbing my windows with no further trouble.

Why had the excitement in the tank ended so abruptly? Why had it begun in the first place?

The question continued to plague me for months. Why this apparently unprovoked attack? I wanted to believe that sharks and people could get along peaceably. Therefore I had to know why the violence happened, so as to know how to avoid it in the future.

"Why don't you talk to Dr. L.J.V. Compagno?" suggested Ed Miller, a friend at Steinhart Aquarium. "He was the white shark scientific consultant for the movie *Jaws* and is the United Nations adviser on the subject of sharks. I'll give him a call, see if he's in the mood for visitors. Watch your step with him, though. If Dr. C. does not like you, he will very definitely let you know."

I pulled my little truck to a halt in a parking lot at the bottom of a hill on the outskirts of Tiburon, a city close to San Francisco that was named after a shark.

Three cars, two obviously abandoned and one looking about to become so, rusted in the sun. A barnlike structure rose before me.

I was nervous, wondering what Dr. L.J.V. Compagno would be like. I had seen one of his papers, "The Phyletic Relationships of Sharks and Rays." It was written mostly in Latin and I couldn't understand it. I was not a scientist. I had some practical experience and I had read a lot, but if someone had asked me what was the difference between a ray and a shark, I would have said that one was flat and the other was not. Compagno had written a whole paper on that subject, containing sentences like: "The neurocranium of rays lacks occipital condyles present in sharks with calcified centra." Which had something to do with head shape. I thought.

Up closer to Dr. Compagno's building I saw the words VENDING/SUPPLIES stenciled in faded paint on the wall beside a rusted screen door. I pulled the screen back—it creaked—and knocked on the wooden door behind it. No answer. I knocked again, louder, and heard a faint disgusted sigh from inside, as if its owner would really rather I just went away. I let the screen door close quickly and stepped back.

The wooden door opened. Behind the rusted screen a white blur resolved into an enormous paint-stained T-shirt. Dr. C. was huge! Not tall, only five ten or so, but he must have weighed two hundred fifty pounds, and he looked like a slightly out-of-training grizzly. His jeans were worn through at the knees, and his shoes were broken.

"Yes?" The black eyes were not encouraging.

"Um, I'm the diver, uh, writer from Marine World?" I stammered.

"I am very busy. I don't know how much time I can give you," said the thirtyish scientist, but he grudgingly stepped aside and let me in.

We stood in a high-ceilinged "living room" furnished with a couch of the sort that might be bought at auction for a dollar, and two chairs that should have been thrown in for the price. Aside from these scant accommodations to comfort, everything had to do with sharks.

Shark models hung from invisible wires, and a plaster mold hinted at more to be built. The walls were shelved to the ceiling, thick with books I recognized and others I did not. At the back the living room opened onto a two-level laboratory, and everywhere were large blue boxes with sharks painted on the side. One of the boxes had car parts on top of it. I puzzled over that for a second, and then let it slip by.

"As I said, I am really very busy," the huge man was telling me again, but I was too absorbed in the scene to listen.

On the wall above him three shark jaws gaped in silent threat. The first two were easy to identify—the notch-edged daggers of the great white and the L-shaped scythes of the tiger are the most distinctive shark teeth of all. But the third set was not quite so simple. The teeth were smallish, clean-sided triangles, evenly shaped top and bottom, once backed by plenty of muscle as could be seen by the heavy framework of cartilage beneath.

"Is that a bull shark, Dr. Compagno?" I guessed, and the scientist smiled, recognizing a fellow shark enthusiast. I wasn't some smart-aleck sensationalist reporter, there to waste his time and write some ripoff trashy article about bloodthirsty monsters of the deep.

"Yes, it is," he said. "Call me Leonard. Take the gray chair, it has the best back."

I settled in for one of the happiest times of my life. I felt completely at home, and I tried to think of the hardest questions I could come up with about sharks. I might never have such an opportunity again.

*   *   *

The first question, of course, was about the attack in the electrical storm. *Could the storm itself* have made the sharks excited?

"It is possible. Studies by Kalmijn and Djigraaf show that sharks are incredibly sensitive to even the faintest electrical impulses, such as those put out by a stingray hiding under the sand. An electrical storm might conceivably be as exciting to sharks as the vibrations of a wounded fish or the scent of blood."

Wow. I knew that was as close to "yes" as any scientist would get without having done or seen research on the subject.

Conversation continued. Leonard Compagno was like a friendly encyclopedia. I was used to being the person in the room who knew most about sharks—but not in this room.

For example, I knew that sharks are often used as food for human consumption, either disguised under other names like whitefish or rock salmon in fish sticks, or out in the open like kamaboko, the Japanese shark pancakes, and quite a few other delicacies. Leonard knew *how much* shark was eaten by people worldwide in a typical year, such as 300,085 metric tons in 1978.

I had wondered about thresher sharks, which have an amazingly long arching upper tail fin, as long as the rest of the shark. It was once thought they beat up whales with this tail. That was obviously not true, but what was that oddly shaped tail really for?

"From eyewitness accounts, and the fact that threshers are frequently caught on hooks imbedded in their tails, it appears the hyperextended caudal fin is used like a buggy whip, to knock out individual fish," said Leonard.

Was there a reliable antishark protection for shipwreck survivors? I knew sharks could individually be killed in an almost endless variety of ways, but what about a shark feeding frenzy when a boat went down at sea and all those poor people were struggling in the water?

"The best defense against a feeding frenzy is not to let it develop in the first place," he told me. "U.S. Navy Captain C. Scott Johnson's antishark screen is designed to do just that. It is nothing more than a heavy plastic bag with inflatable rings attached to the open end, to make it float, but it could save lives. The person in danger blows up the float rings with a few breaths of air, fills the ring-topped bag with water, climbs inside, and *virtually disappears from the sharks*. All the signals that excite sharks to frenzy—the scent of blood or body waste, vibrations of thrashing limbs in the water, even the natural electricity of living tissue—are gone, blocked off by the antishark screen. And the whole thing can be folded up flat as a handkerchief and put in the pocket of a life preserver."

Did he think shark attacks were increasing down the California coast in the infamous "Red Corridor," north and south around Monterey Bay, which has been called the most dangerous shark attack area in the world?

"No. I have all the shark attacks in the 'Red Corridor' since 1933 on computer, and there has been a grand total of four fatalities. Obviously nobody wants to be one of those people, but the risk of death on the highway to the beach is much greater. Fifty thousand people die on the roads in America each year, compared to a worldwide total of maybe ten or twelve fatalities by shark."

What about the sea lion population down near Monterey? Did their presence automatically put divers in life-and-death danger, since white sharks ate sea lions and would therefore be nearby?

"David Allen, an archeologist, has been scuba diving three months out of the year for five years in Algoa Bay, South Africa, in the nearly constant presence of white sharks. There is a colony of giant southern fur seals there, very similar to California's Steller's sea lions, and the white sharks are naturally interested in them. As many as ten white sharks, ten to eighteen feet long, have been seen in the area at once. The divers only dive when the water is clear enough so they will not be mistaken for seals, and the white sharks go about their business.

"The first year the divers got scared and used a bang stick (a shotgun shell in a pipe) to kill one white when it swam near, but after that they realized the sharks were not trying to eat the people, and the two species got along. The divers witnessed the white sharks preying upon the seals, and one diver even tried to tug a killed seal away from a white shark that had the animal in its mouth. Obviously that is not something one recommends, but it does show a degree of restraint on the white shark's part. Imagine trying to do something similar with an African lion, for instance!

"But in any event, there it is: divers, white sharks, and marine mammal prey, all in the water together, and the people remaining unharmed. I see no reason why Monterey should be considered significantly different, and statistics show that it is not. Divers are in more danger from crossing the street to get to the beach than they are from the white sharks of Monterey."

A question I wish I had raised with Leonard Compagno is, Would a study of the shark's immune system help us in the battle against AIDS (acquired immune deficiency syndrome)? The virus that causes AIDS attacks and often destroys a person's immune system, leaving him or her unable to fight off a host of fatal diseases. As yet there is no cure. Sharks, with their ability to eat diseased fish and not become sick themselves, have a wonderfully strong immune system. If we understood more about it, we might find some clues for understanding and conquering AIDS.

Leonard opened one of the blue boxes for me. Inside was a preserved tiger shark, orange eye still looking furious in death. Beside it was a cookie cutter shark, two feet long, with surprisingly enormous teeth under lips like suction cups. It used the lips to glom onto the sides of whales before nipping out a circular snack. There was a smooth-skinned silky shark, and one I'd never heard of, a false cat shark with whiskers and marks like rippling light across its back.

People sent Leonard boxed sharks in the mail. This made for some interesting trips to the airport and some tense explanations to the customs officials, who might not be inclined to believe there was a six-foot Indian saw shark inside a lengthy box.

" 'Open it,' the customs man said, and I did," said Leonard, grinning. "The formaldehyde gassed out half the airport. He let me close the box back up then."

Leonard showed me drawers filled with dozens of different sets of shark teeth, and an enormous red book which was his doctoral thesis, a 932-page paper on the order of sharks called the carcharinoids, which includes about two hundred species. He was about to leave for Africa, where he would be completing a ten-year project—the scientific classification of every known species of shark in the world.

I had a couple of stories for Leonard as well. Like the one about the aquarium worker who stuck his arm down the throat of a refrigerated white shark and could not pull it out, shark teeth pointing inward as they do. Since a person with a frozen shark on his arm cannot live a full and useful life, the man had to reach a hot-water hose and spray the shark's thick jaw muscles. When they relaxed, he got loose.

We had both heard the one about the "mighty" hunter who caught a little leopard shark and stuffed a hand grenade down its throat and set it loose, just for the sadistic pleasure of watching the animal explode. It was only justice when the shark swam right back under the fisherman's boat and sank it when the hand grenade went off.

But as we recalled the mako shark that leaped eighteen feet to get the blood-dripping body of an executed criminal hung over the entrance to a harbor, as reported by French scientist Lacépède in 1798, I looked out the window and saw it was dark. I looked at my watch. I had stayed five hours!

As I got up, I wished there was something I could give Leonard to thank him for the visit. But what? He would have every book on sharks that I had, and I could not help him with a great dream of his—that of founding a shark research institute. Then I had an idea.

"Leonard, have you ever been underwater with sharks?"

"No."

"Can you dive?"

Again the massive head swung side to side.

"Can you remember to keep breathing underwater—because if you hold a breath of compressed air while swimming upward you could embolize and die?" (Meaning that a bubble of air might expand in the bloodstream and block the flow of blood to the brain with fatal results.)

Leonard nodded. He would remember to keep breathing.

*   *   *

Two weeks later a white-shirted giant stood in the flume, bending over with his face underwater, practicing breathing with a regulator in his mouth. None of our wet suits fit the 5'10½", 250-pound shark scientist, so he would just have to be cold. He was about to go underwater with sharks for the very first time in his life. In the laboratory Leonard was a master. Here, he was an absolute novice.

He dog-paddled out to the middle of the reeftank and sank where I pointed. Down he went, emitting great clouds of bubbles. When he hit the floor, he lost his balance and sat down hard. But he got right up, enduring the strangeness of breathing air underwater on the first scuba dive of his life. The sharks came over to investigate.

I stayed right next to Leonard, watching him, watching them.

He stood in that spot watching sharks close up for more than an hour, long past the point when his skin became covered with goosebumps. He had begun to shiver, but he didn't want to leave when I pulled his arm. I did not actually have to drag him out, but he was sure in no hurry. I watched to make certain he kept breathing when he rose, and he did.

"That water is pretty cold, huh?" I asked as Leonard's teeth chattered behind lips that looked numb and blue.

"I was not conscious of the temperature," he said. "That was of no consequence. To be close with the sharks under living conditions was more than I ever expected. They are so different, alive in their element and under their own power. So . . . beautiful. And that big one actually made an exploratory pass at me, I am sure of it. Don't you think?"

I nodded, having seen it too. Not being a diver, he had been a little clumsy, and his big white calves had flashed like the bellies of wounded fish. Several of the sharks, including Sevengill herself, had come over to check him out.

"You liked it?"

He pushed his black hair off his forehead. His eyes were shining and his face was alight with a gigantic wondering smile.

"It was like the first time I ever saw a grove of giant redwood trees, and saw the sunbeams coming down from the leaves so far above," he said. "I felt that same sense of mystery, and reverence for life."

The Two-Thousand-
and-First Dive

8

By 1984 I had been diving professionally for almost thirteen years: six hundred fifty work weeks, three thousand two hundred fifty diving days. Typically, a Marine World diver makes two dives a day, doing heavy scrubbing for two and a half hours in the morning and something lighter for an hour and a half in the afternoon. Of that estimated six thousand dives (knocking off five hundred lazy afternoons when I did paperwork instead of getting wet), I would guess at least a third were spent in the presence of sharks.

In all those hours underwater, often with the sharks, the ratio of violence to peace was like an exclamation point in the middle of a giant sheet of otherwise unmarked paper. Violence might be what we remembered most, the times when everything went wrong, but peace between sharks and people was the day-to-day reality.

The more I studied sharks, the more I believed this was the

case all over the world. Every time somebody said, oh, this shark is the most dangerous or that place is the most terrible for attack, somebody else would turn right around and either disprove it or show how the danger could be dealt with.

People have called white sharks the most dangerous beasts in the world, yet archeologist David Allen's dives with the seal colony and great whites in Africa proved that white sharks can coexist peacefully with people, assuming clear water and folks who keep their wits about them. Of course, anything with teeth must be regarded as dangerous and treated accordingly. A white shark as long as a station wagon can never be a creature to ignore.

Some sharks like the tiger, once thought to be fury incarnate (and definitely dangerous in certain circumstances), have proved to actually be of moderate character. The tiger shark is now sometimes used undrugged in motion-picture work.

Jacques Cousteau, the man I respect most in the world, called the oceanic whitetip (which looks a great deal like a deep-ocean sevengill) "the most dangerous shark," and I agree, yet neither that champion of the sea nor any of his co-workers has ever been harmed by even this aggressive shark. The great photography team Ron and Valerie Taylor have filmed cageless in the feeding frenzy of those same oceanic whitetips. A whale had died and the sharks were eating it, and the Taylors swam right up to the whale and filmed the oncoming sharks. They had to fight as I had done during the electrical storm, continually bonking every shark who came near, but they survived.

Even the horror of a mass shark feeding frenzy against ocean-stranded people could now be prevented, if somebody would manufacture the Johnson Antishark Screen that Leonard Compagno told me about—that simple plastic bag with a floatable ring top which lets people inside disappear from the senses of the shark. If I had my way, it would be illegal for any ship or plane to cross the ocean without a Johnson Antishark Screen folded in the pocket of every life preserver.

The problems between sharks and people can be worked out. In whatever part of the sea people dive, the habits of sharks who live there can be learned and understood.

As usual, it is Cousteau who put it best. "Sharks can be handled," I heard him say on a TV talk show. This pretty much sums it up. As Dr. Compagno indicated, sharks are dangerous but by taking simple precautions, the danger can be almost totally eliminated.

By diving with people who know the local area, you can be prepared for whatever problems lie ahead of you, from the more usual difficulties like heavy surf to the habits of the sharks of that neighborhood.

If you went diving in a tropical reef and saw a whitetip reef shark swimming awkwardly, fins pointing down, body arched stiff and clumsy-looking, the experienced diver with you would know to back off, that the shark was protecting its territory.

A bull shark lifting its "lips," exposing its teeth, and shaking its head is an animal that is nervous and threatening, and a sensible person would pause and slow down and calmly retreat.

Certain things no diver should ever do, and they could add up to a long list, but what they boil down to is: Don't act like shark food. Swim calmly; don't thrash around on the surface like a wounded fish. Let sharks own the ocean at night, when they most actively feed, unless you are a very experienced diver and are with a group. Don't swim without a swimsuit in the sea;

statistics show nude swimmers are more frequently victims. Per-haps patches of untanned skin remind a shark of a fish's stomach, which normally never shows unless the fish is in trouble. Neither should anyone wear jewelry underwater, because of its glittery flash. Nor should spearfishers tie their kill to their waist—what a place for shark bait to be attached!

But sharks in general are reasonable creatures, except when we teach them to be otherwise—by exciting them with buckets of blood for moviemaking purposes, or by burying people in the water without coffins, which still happens in some sections of the world. In Lake Nicaragua and portions of the Nile and Zambezi rivers, it is literally not safe to swim. The bull (also called the cub, pilot, or Zambezi) shark is deadly dangerous there because for hundreds of years corpses have been put in the water. This is teaching sharks to eat people. The same species of shark, *Carcharhinus leucas*, swims up North American rivers and to my knowledge has never attacked a person there, probably because it does not routinely encounter dead bodies.

Even in the most desperate freak situations there are ways to win out. An Arab fisherman sitting on a low dock, splashing his feet in the water, suddenly found a giant shark taking both his legs in its cavern of a mouth. But the old fisherman calmly stuck his thumbs in the great shark's *nostrils*, and lived to point out the scars to his children.

The simple truth is that shark attack is about the rarest imag-inable cause of death among humans. Farm animals kill more people than sharks ever do. My wife's grandmother saw a farmer fall into a pigpen and get killed and partly eaten by the snuffling hogs. Even deer can become fiercely aggressive during mating season. Almost any large animal you can name, and some very small ones, too, are more likely than sharks to hurt people. Even bee stings and dog bites can be deadly serious threats. It has been estimated that you are three times more likely to be struck by lightning than to ever be attacked by a shark. By comparison, shark attack is an astonishingly minimal risk.

There are nearly three million certified scuba divers in America alone. Almost none will ever even get to *see* a shark, let alone be bothered by one.

There is danger undersea as there is danger on the land, but the real horror goes away when people put on a face mask and take a good look underwater. What is most frightening is the unknown, discovering suddenly deep water beneath your feet, being dunked underwater and blinded by saltwater, and you wait for something to rise and snatch your scrabbling, helpless legs. . . . But with mask, swim fins, and an air tank, you are not helpless anymore. You are a large and powerful ocean animal, one of the biggest and toughest creatures in the sea.

If you had spent those two thousand dives side by side with me and the sharks, you might have been tempted to think, as I did, that shark attack as a genuine risk could be completely forgotten.

And yet there is always the possibility of that two-thousand-and-first shark dive.

I was working alone in the reeftank that morning when the shark took my head in its mouth.

There was no warning that I could detect. One moment I was vacuum-brushing the floor and the next a vise squeezed in around my skull. I heard the grate of teeth on bone; my head was shaken back and forth so hard my spine cracked like knuckles popping. Then the pressure ceased. I was let go.

Disbelieving, I touched hesitant fingers up to the blue rubber hood, felt the edges of the severed cloth and rubber.

I did not know why I was grabbed, or why I was released. Perhaps the taste was unappetizing. But there was no question who had done it. Only one shark in the tank had jaws large enough to slip easily around the mass of a human head.

I saw her, Sevengill, twenty feet away, turning, coming back. She was 7'9" long now and exceptionally girthy through the brown- and black-spotted torso; Sevengill was in her muscular prime. I hated every inch and pound of her right then. Rage and embarrassment pulsated through me, like a red tide rising. Why had I not felt the attack building up? And why had she done this to me? So many times I had defended her against those who called sharks monsters, and now for her to bite me when my back was turned—this was not fair!

I was on the floor in the usual semi-pushup position that we used when cleaning. Letting the vacuum hose float away, I rose to my feet, cursing at Sevengill in my mind. My weight belt dropped from my chest to my knees. I had forgotten I was wearing the heavy lead weights high in the armpits to minimize back strain, and I had to fumble madly to haul the belt up to my waist and tighten the buckle before Sevengill got near.

I knew her body language well enough now to recognize Sevengill's moods. The gold-black eyeball flickered in and out uncertainly; the head motion was tentative, unsure; she was changing her mind. I could have raised up my arms to make myself look bigger, or moved quickly toward her, or done anything threatening and she would have gone away. Or I could have just stood still, and she would almost certainly have swum around me.

For a moment I did nothing, and she started to move off in a different direction, apparently realizing there was no food for her here. But I did not want her to leave. Not now, not after what she had done. I wanted to get even.

I tricked her. I wiggled the fingers of my left hand like a wounded fish flopping, the way I did when I wanted to call her to come and be fed. Sevengill still hesitated, but she came over anyway.

I punched her just as hard as I could, connecting with the side of her head, just above the left nostril. It was an uneducated punch, without skill or science, but I never hit anything harder. Every ounce of my now two-hundred-twenty-pound ex-weight-lifter's body (and considerable emotion) went into that blow. I socked so hard the muscles of my forearm cramped up from the impact, and she slammed against the wall, ricocheted off the floor, and was gone.

The wound on my head was not worth a Band-Aid: a few pinprick incisions, a headache for a few hours, nothing more. But I was furious with Sevengill. Even when I looked at my wet-suit hood and understood the reason for the bite, I could not forgive her.

The hood was old, almost worn out, and it had ripped before. I had sewn it back together with fishline but not too well, and the red inner lining showed like a wound. A piece of scarlet cloth had worked loose and had apparently been flapping back and forth, like a piece of torn flesh.

The shark had only done what any predator does. She had seen something that looked wounded and had given it an investigatory mouthing. She had not bitten hard; I knew from the white shark she had killed and the smaller sevengill she had bitten in half that she had the strength to bite through cartilage, and probably bone. Shark jaw closing power has been measured in the *tons* of pressure per square inch. She could conceivably have shaken and cut right through my skull.

I could not trust her anymore. I glared at the shark when I passed by the windows and could never completely relax in the shark tank again.

I had thought I had shark attack all figured out, that sharks could be lived with. Was I wrong? Again and again I worried the facts in my mind, shaking them back and forth as the shark had shaken my head.

Logically I knew the incident did not contradict what I believed. Sharks will behave like sharks, like the predators they are. The attack was almost insignificant compared to the multitude of opportunities she had had to do much worse before.

I knew all this, just as surely as I knew that both my children will become divers, which I would not allow if I thought the ocean was not safe for them.

But still I could take no more joy in Sevengill's presence. I felt betrayed, as if a friend had given me pain. I thought we had some kind of understanding, that maybe she recognized me and would never do such a thing to me.

I did not worry at first when Sevengill went off her feed. It was normal for the sharks to slow down their eating in the heat of summer, and 1984 was warm. As the water temperature rose in San Francisco Bay, which supplied our water, so did the temperature in the reeftank.

The canvas shade tarp over the tank was getting ragged and shabby-looking, and Marine World's management decided we should remove the tarp. Apparently no one in authority considered what a rise in heat might mean to temperature-sensitive sharks. Divers are no part of the Marine World power structure, and I was not even told about the decision until the day the tarp was cut off. Afterward I squawked, but not effectively enough to get another (admittedly highly expensive) shade tarp put up. To be fair, many aquariums have had success with unshaded tanks, so it is not that management did not care about what was best for the animals. But there can be no question it was a mistake.

Sevengill died. In my opinion the heat of the unshaded tank did it. We found her lying still on the bottom of the reef aquarium tank. At first I could not believe it was her.

The shark was lying on her side. Her gill area showed red. A section of flesh and cartilage had been removed from her head and neck. It wasn't the wound that had killed her, though, I realized numbly as I touched the rough-skinned body. That just finished her off. No shark in the tank and few indeed in the ocean would have dared to mess with her if she had been healthy.

Diver Alan Therkelsen removed Sevengill's jaws, mounted them on black cloth and board, and gave them to me as a gift. I also took her tail, with its top portion so much longer than the lower section, as is usual for sharks, and salted and dried it, then tacked it to a board. This was unusual for me. I do not hunt and would not have allowed a stuffed animal in the house. I told myself I just wanted the jaws and tail fin to show to schoolchildren when I went out and gave lectures, but that was not the truth. I just did not want to be parted from Sevengill, not completely. Everything seemed wrong. I could not even grieve properly.

When an animal dies, one that I have been close to, I usually go off somewhere alone and remember, trying to relive in some small way the times we had together, good and bad, the excitements and peaceful moments, wrapping up the life we had together. I get teary-eyed for a while, or maybe kick my desk.

But now I could not settle what had happened, could not get it straight in my mind. I felt incomplete, as though I had been given all the pieces of a puzzle except one. I still felt bad toward Sevengill, as though she had betrayed me, let me down. I knew I was not getting something, missing out on an important chance to understand.

And then one day the lions and the tigers fought.

Trainer Ron Whitfield was working his usual act, with the all-male tiger and lion group mounted on a pyramid. At Ron's signal Thai the tiger came down as he had done a thousand times before, but this time he sank his teeth into the leg of a lion named Notch. Notch turned around quick as lightning, knocked the tiger over, and bit into its belly. Immediately Beau, Notch's brother, leaped over to help, and suddenly every lion and tiger in the ring remembered past arguments the trainer had not let them settle. With a noise like a freight-train collision, the high-fenced arena shook under the hurtling impact of fighting lions and tigers.

Whole big-cat acts have died in such battles before, killing each other off and the victors then dying of the wounds. Sometimes the trainers have been killed as well. But Whitfield would not leave the arena. Snatching a broomstick, he waded into the tangle of roaring, fighting quarter-ton cats, whacking right and left, while outside the arena wife Roxanne and assistant Pat Flora got busy with a fire hose and a carbon dioxide fire extinguisher, startling the lions and thereby saving the tigers, who had much the worst of the fight.

I sought out Ron Whitfield some time afterward. I knew he trained the modern way, avoiding the staged and destructive fights which had once been a part of wild animal acts, and I wanted to ask him a question that had a special meaning to me. I wanted to know if the trainer felt sad that he had been unable to train the savagery out of the animals.

His answer surprised me.

"If you truly love an animal," said Whitfield, "you must love it for what it is, not for what you would want it to be."

I felt a sort of click, as if the missing puzzle piece had fitted into place.

This was really a basic principle of living with animals, and I had gotten into trouble in my feelings for Sevengill when I forgot it.

For if Sevengill was absolutely no monster, neither was she on this earth to be my pet.

The shark was a force of nature, like a mountain or a storm. My perception of her had changed, but she herself had not changed, except perhaps in learning to associate me with the availability of food because I fed her. She was neither my friend nor my enemy. She was like the sea itself, a positive part of the natural world, to be respected.

When she mouthed my hood, she was performing her natural job, investigating what might be something sick or wounded. I fought back, reacting as a healthy ocean animal would, and the incident was over, except for my emotional reaction. I got my feelings hurt, which was foolish.

If the shark were not a reliable predator, it would not help keep the ocean so alive and vigorous. By eating the weak and wounded, sharks keep the fish population from outgrowing the food supply and then starving. By eating the sick, sharks prevent disease from spreading. Sharks are more than just the bringers of the end; they are also the givers of life.

Sevengill lived and died by the predator's law. When she in her turn had grown weak, a shark had come for her, bringing a mercifully swift end to life, as she had brought it to others.

The sorrow that I felt now had lost its edge of bitterness. What mattered was not that the shark had died, but that she had lived, and lived well.

Now I had Sevengill back as she was meant to be, fixed forever in my memory as she was at her best. I could remember her now as she had been on one perfect spring afternoon, when the water in the reef was exceptionally clear. The filtration equipment must have been working very well; every particle of algae seemed to be gone. It was as though we swam in air.

Across the middle of the tank she came, moving with that peculiar combination of modesty and majesty which marked her always. Her mouth was slightly open; she breathed in the sea.

And then something small and wonderful happened, a phenomenon I had never seen before with a sevengill. Was it a trick of illumination, or a natural oil on the denticle points of her hide? I do not know. But on her skin the light refracted, breaking into color.

As if the ocean wished to bless a humble creature, there was a faint but unmistakable rainbow around her.

For Further Reading

BUDKER, PAUL. *The Life of Sharks*. Columbia University Press, 1971.
My personal favorite of the technical shark books. Tough reading in
places, and occasionally outdated, but fascinating material.

CLARK, EUGENIE. *The Lady and the Sharks*. Harper & Row, 1969.
The story of Ms. Clark's experiences as founder of Florida's Cape Haze
Marine Laboratory. The author's love of sea life shines through.

COUSTEAU, JACQUES-YVES & PHILLIPPE. *The Shark: Splendid Savage of the
Sea*. Doubleday, 1970.
The story of a shark expedition by the Cousteau team. Includes Captain
Cousteau's most frightening shark encounter.

ELLIS, RICHARD. *The Book of Sharks*. Harcourt Brace Jovanovich, 1975.
A classic in the field, combining the author's fine paintings, many photographs, and wide-ranging, readable information.

LINEAWEAVER, THOMAS H., III, and BACKUS, RICHARD H. *The Natural History of Sharks*. Anchor Natural History Books, Doubleday, 1973.
A very thorough book, touching on virtually all aspects of sharks. Lots of
good stories too.

TAYLOR, RON and VALERIE, editors. *Great Shark Stories*. Harper & Row,
1978 (hardcover); Bantam, 1978 (paperback).
The editors were the photographers for the real white shark footage in
such movies as *Jaws*, and their book lives up to its title.

WATKINS, ANTHONY. *The Sea My Hunting Ground*. St. Martin's Press, 1960.
What harpooning basking sharks for a living is like. Well-written and
interesting, but kind of sad.

Index

great mako shark, 16, 107
great white shark, 29–39, 60, 82, 102, 104–105, 111, 117
Greene, Norval, 44, 73–74
groupers, 27, 93

horn sharks, 29

immune system, 28, 105–106
Indian saw shark, 106
intelligence, 80–81, 89, 98

Jaws, 30, 37, 100
jaws, 12, 19, 23, 50, 75, 114–116, 118
Johnson, Captain C. Scott, 104, 111–112

kamaboko, 103
kelp bass, 29, 37, 69–70, 94
killer whale, 32, 60

Lacépède, 107
lateral line, 5, 17, 39
lemon shark, 61
leopard shark, 14–16, 29, 40, 41, 91–92
liver, 13

McCosker, Dr. John, 73
Marine World/Africa USA, 20–21, 26, 31, 58–59
mating, 12
meat, shark, 100, 103
mermaid purses, 29
metal, shark's sensitivity to, 18, 50, 82
Monterey Bay, 104
moray eel, 37, 77, 94
mud shark, 4–7

Notorynchus cepedianus, ix, 44
Notorynchus maculatus, 43–44
nurse shark, 22–24, 40, 63

oceanic whitetip shark, 111
orca, 60

Pacific mackerel, 14, 74–77, 88, 98
personality, 77, 78–85
pilot shark, 113
plankton, 18, 67
Powell, Dave, 41

rabbitfish, 14
"Red Corridor," 104
reef aquarium tank, 24–27, 29, 118

safety precautions with sharks, 15, 37, 55, 56, 75, 96, 112–113
San Francisco Bay, 3, 4, 16
scales, 6
Schneiderian folds, 17
sea bass, 27, 28–29
sea lions, 10–12, 59–60, 104
seals, 59, 105, 111
sea turtles, 29, 32, 74–75, 76, 83
sevengill shark, ix, 3–19
    aggressiveness, 41, 43–44
    birth, 3–7
    description of, 16–17, 39, 50, 98–99
    feeding habits, 12, 14, 39, 68–70, 71, 72–73
    gills, 4, 6
    heat, sensitivity to, 118–119
    pups, 3, 6, 7–16
    speed, 11, 16, 49, 99
    teeth, 12, 16–17, 41, 90–91
shark stick, 32, 35, 65, 74
shark transport box, 19, 41
size, 42
skeleton, 6, 42
skin, shark's, 33–34, 52, 65
skin teeth, 6, 33, 86
spiny dogfish shark, 4, 29
Steinhart Aquarium, 19, 38–39, 40–41, 72
stingray, 17, 71–72
striped bass, 29, 73
swimming, shark's, 12, 66, 80

Taylor, Ron and Valerie, 111
teeth, 33, 35, 90, 102, 106–107, 112
thresher shark, 103
tiger shark, 66, 102, 106, 111
Torpedo nobiliana, 78–79
torpedo ray, 78–79

"walking" sharks, 31–34
whitetop reef shark, 112

Zambezi shark, 113

Index 125

DON C. REED

took up scuba diving as a second choice after weightlifting and, after completing diving school, became a diver at Marine World/Africa USA near San Francisco. His experiences there with a variety of sea creatures over a thirteen-year period provided the material not only for this book but also for an adult book, *Notes from an Underwater Zoo*, and a number of magazine articles for adults and young readers. During Marine World's recent, temporary close pending completion of new quarters in Vallejo, California, Mr. Reed finished the requirements for a bachelor's degree in English from California State College at Hayward. He lives in Fremont, California, with his wife, Jeannie, and his children, Desirée, age 14, and Roman, age 11.